Following Narnia®

Writing Lessons in Structure and Style

by
Laura Bettis

Teacher's Manual

Second Edition, February 2013
Institute for Excellence in Writing, L.L.C.

Also by Laura Bettis:
Following Narnia® Writing Lessons in Structure and Style Student Book

The purchase of this book entitles its owner to a free downloadable copy of
The Student Resource Notebook.
Go to IEW.com/FN-E

Copyright Policy

Following Narnia
Writing Lessons in Structure and Style
Second Edition, February 2013

Copyright © 2012 Laura Bettis

ISBN: 978-1-62341-000-1

Our duplicating/copying policy for this **Teacher's Manual**:

All rights reserved.

No part of this book may be reproduced, stored in a retrieval system, or transmitted in any form or by any means, electronic, mechanical, photocopying, recording, or otherwise, without the prior written permission of the author, except as provided by U.S.A. copyright law and the specific policy below:

Home use: You may copy student-related materials from this Teacher's Manual as well as the accompanying Student Book for use by multiple children within your immediate family.

Small group or co-op classes: Each teacher is required to have his or her own Teacher's Manual and one copy of the Student Book. You may copy student-related materials from the Teacher's Manual for use in your class. You may not copy from the Student Book. Each participating student or family is required to purchase a Student Book.

Classroom teachers: Each teacher is required to have his or her own Teacher's Manual and one copy of the Student Book. You may copy student-related materials from the Teacher's Manual for use in your class. You may not copy from the Student Book. Each participating student is required to purchase his or her own Student Book.

Library use: Printed materials may be checked out of a lending library provided patrons agree not to make copies.

Institute for Excellence in Writing
8799 N. 387 Road
Locust Grove, OK 74352
800.856.5815
IEW.com
Printed in the United States of America

Accessing Your Download

The purchase of this book entitles its owner to a free download of the optional *Student Resource Notebook e-book* (110 pages*).

To download your complimentary e-book, please follow the directions below:

1. Go to our website, IEW.com
2. Sign in to your online customer account. If you do not have an account, you will need to create one.
3. After you are logged in, go to this web page: IEW.com/FN-E
4. Click on the red download arrow.
5. You will be taken to your File Downloads page. Click on the file name, and the e-book will download onto your computer.

Please note: You are free to download and print this e-book resource as many times as needed for use within *your immediate family or classroom*. However, this information is proprietary, and we are trusting you to be on your honor not to share it with anyone. Please see the copyright page for further details. Thank you.

*If you would prefer to purchase the *Student Resource Notebook* as a preprinted, spiral-bound book, it is available at IEW.com/SRN-B

If you have any difficulty receiving this download after going through the steps above, please call 800.856.5815.

Institute for Excellence in Writing
8799 N. 387 Road
Locust Grove, OK 74352

Introduction

Thank you for purchasing
Following Narnia Writing Lesson in Structure and Style.

Main Purpose of This Book: The intent of *Following Narnia* is to help you see how you can integrate the IEW techniques with your other subjects. Your student will write on topics from the Narnia stories, but also from history and science, while using all of the IEW structural models.

Course Prerequisite: The teacher/parent should have viewed the *Teaching Writing: Structure & Style* (TWSS) DVDs or attended a live TWSS workshop with Andrew Pudewa. Have your TWSS syllabus handy as you go through these assignments with your student. There are notations on which TWSS disc you can refer to, along with the corresponding page numbers in the TWSS syllabus should you need further instruction. *There is no prerequisite for the student.

Schedule: The lessons are designed to be taught once a week. After teaching the lesson, students will use the rest of the week to write, edit, and rewrite. Allow the student extra time if needed.

Teacher's Manual: The Teacher's Manual is a necessary component to this course, as it will guide the teacher/parent through each lesson in the Student Book. There are in-depth explanations, tips, and other notes that will ensure that you and your student are successful with *Following Narnia*. Always read the teacher instructions for each lesson beforehand to familiarize yourself with the lesson and any new material being introduced. The TWSS DVDs are the primary training for all IEW programs; review them as necessary.

Reading *The Chronicles of Narnia*: Listed at the beginning of each lesson is a reading assignment, which may be completed while the student works on the writing lesson.

Analyzing Words: Students will analyze some of the words that C.S. Lewis selected and put into the Narnia stories. The Teacher's Manual contains the list of words and which chapter they came from. Please read all of the instructions for a more thorough explanation of this wonderful option.

Checklists: *Following Narnia* comes with two different sets of checklists. The Student Book has checklists that correspond with each lesson, and they are located at the back. An optional set of customizable checklists that correspond to the IEW structural units is located at the back of the Teacher's Manual. The customizable checklists allow you and the student to control the requirements, so that they are required to use all of the stylistic techniques they have found to be **easy, plus one** more they are learning. **EZ+1.**

The ultimate goal is for students to memorize and own the information on the checklist, so that they will be able to mentally run through the checklist in their mind when doing any writing assignment; not because those items appear on a checklist, but because that is how one writes well.

Writing is a form of communication, an extension of thought, an expression of individual creativity. This course is designed to help you teach your children how to write well. Now let's begin the comings and goings between Narnia and our world.

Laura Bettis

Table of Contents / Scope and Sequence

The Student Book contains checklists specific to each lesson. The customizable checklists are included in the Teacher's Manual as an option.

5 paragraphs

8 paragraphs

The Magician's Nephew

Lesson	Writing Topic		Chapter for Reading Assignment
1	Sherlock Holmes	3	1
2	Atlantis	13	2–4
3	Jadis Tells a Story	15	5
4	Sister Tells a Story	17	6
5	London	19	7
6	Parliament	19	
7	Palace of Westminster	19	8
8	Buckingham Palace	19	
9	A Lamp-Post Is Planted	21	9
10	Primrose, Buttercups, Daisies	23	10–12
11	The Crown Jewels of England		13–15

Teacher Notes: Lesson 1

Structure: IEW Unit 1 – Key Word Outlines and Unit 2 – Summarizing from Notes
Style: banned words
Topics: Sherlock Holmes, Sidney Padget, Sir Arthur Conan Doyle
Student Reading Assignment: *The Magician's Nephew*, Chapter 1

The goals of this lesson:
- To show students how to take notes from what they've read without writing down *every* word.
- To teach students public speaking skills as they "tell back" information using only their outlines to remind them of what they read.
- To teach students a powerful study technique.
- To show students how to turn outline notes into a paragraph.
- For students to become confident and independent in the process of summarizing information using only their notes (without copying word-for-word from the source).
- To bring attention to students' word choices by introducing them to the idea of style.

"Always use source texts that are at or below the students' reading level.

Write three key words per line.

Use pen, not pencil."

Lesson 1 includes three paragraphs to practice Units 1 and 2. Take the time needed if IEW is new to you or them. Otherwise, Lesson 1 could be completed in one week.

Remember to review your copy of the Student Book as well as this Teacher's Manual before each lesson. While there are copies of the source texts included in this Teacher's Manual, there is still much information in the Student Book that you need to be aware of as you go through each lesson. Review the lesson in both books beforehand.

IEW Unit 1—Key Word Outlines

For this first lesson, there is more information here in the Teacher's Manual than you will tell your student. Most of this information is for *you* to learn and understand. Review ahead of time, and highlight the things you want to point out to your student. Begin by reading the entire source document together out loud.

 Paragraph 1 from the Student Book

Sherlock Holmes

Sherlock Holmes was a famous investigator in some of the most memorable detective stories ever written. The fictional character was born in 1854 in London, England. Details of his family are few and are hardly mentioned in any of the stories. Holmes liked classical music and the opera. He was observant, intelligent, and alert. He was also very good with disguises, which he used all the time while investigating crimes.

- Talk about key words, and help them find three for each sentence.

Explain that you are going to show them how to take some notes on this information. Begin the paragraph again, and read one sentence. Talk to them about picking out key words. They may pick three words only. **They may use numbers, abbreviations, or simple symbols, and then they are still allowed three actual words as well.** Put a comma between each word or symbol. Repeat this with each sentence, and encourage the students to contribute to the process. Ask them *what they think* is important or interesting. They will enjoy hearing you say, "What do you think is interesting?"

Model the note-taking on a wipe-off, chalkboard, or even a piece of paper while the student writes on his own paper. It is fine if the younger students just copy what you have on the board at this point. They will feel more comfortable with it as they practice. Right now you are teaching a *process*, and some students may need more time to become Independent.

(TWSS Disc 1, *Scene Selection 1,* Unit 1: Note Making and Outlines. View about 7 min. Syllabus pp. 5–7)

 Younger students may use a highlighter to pick out words. Do not let them highlight *phrases*. Highlight individual words only. Onto the outline they should transfer only the key words they choose. Younger siblings who cannot write yet may do this orally with you and will greatly benefit.

Here is a sample key word outline (KWO) for paragraph 1. There are many possibilities, but this will give you an idea. For this first paragraph, the students have a sample KWO in their books. Model for them on the board or on paper, while coaxing as many words from them as possible.

I.   Sherlock Holmes,   famous,   detective

    1.   fictional,   b. 1854,   London

    2.   details,   family,   few

    3.   liked,   ♫ ,   opera

    4.   observant,   intelligent,   alert

    5.   disguises,   investigating,   crimes

FAQ: Why the Roman numeral?

Answer: Each Roman numeral denotes a new paragraph. Each paragraph is a unit of thought and a distinct topic within a bigger subject. Right now you are teaching the *basics* of note-taking from a single source about one topic, which will become one paragraph. Later, the student will learn to take notes where there are several topics; the student will use more Roman numerals: one for each new topic or paragraph.

- Test the outline.

An important step here (and one that is often overlooked) is to tell back or test the outline. This step is multifaceted and very powerful. Telling back, or "testing," the outline will show the student if he chose good words to remind him of the information. Students will learn to select more carefully, the more they practice testing the outlines.

When testing the outline, the student should look at the first line of his notes, think about the information, and then look up from the paper and speak to the audience using a complete sentence. Then he may look back down, review the information on the second line, formulate the thought, and look up and speak to the audience using a complete sentence. He should not read directly from the outline but look up and make eye contact with the audience. Students should not be speaking while looking down at their notes. Continue this for the entire outline. Train students to be effective oral as well as written communicators. Think: *speech preparation.*

(TWSS Disc 1, *Scene Selection 2,* On Public Speaking. View about 7 min. Syllabus p. 8)

A Word on Studying

As a study technique, telling back the outline can be very powerful, and students can use this technique throughout their educational career and in most subjects. Explaining back information that was just read or just heard will help cement the ideas in the brain.

The average person will remember information differently depending on the variation of input.

➤ Consider the following statistics:

If one were only to …	One might remember approximately
see information or **read** it in a book	10–15%
hear information from a lecture or CD	20–25%
see information and **hear** information	30–40%

This is how most people study: They read or listen and jot down some notes. Then they leave the lecture hall or close the notebook, not looking at it again until they need to study for the test. At that time, they look over their notes with scrunched eyebrows, not likely to remember very much.

An effective technique for studying material is: Right after the lecture is over, or after the DVD is finished, or after the student has completed the chapter, go and explain the information to someone else. Teaching and explaining to someone else forces the brain to recall, connect, and verbalize the information in a way that someone else will understand. This results in the speaker's own brain retaining much more of the original content and on a much richer level.

Active — If the student were to teach or tell back the information, he will remember close to **80–90%** of the material. Teaching this technique to your students now will be doing them a great service. Establish this habit with all of their educational pursuits, and they will reap great rewards in their studies!

More information on this topic can be found on IEW's DVD: *Advanced Communication Series*.

The technique of telling back or teaching someone else can be used with even the youngest of students, even if they cannot write yet. The process is teaching them how to learn *actively*.

After they tell back their outline, ask your students if they think they took good notes. Did they remember what everything meant? As they read aloud, did everything flow together and make sense? Enforcing this step now will help them develop the habit of evaluating themselves by listening to their own voice and evaluating their own note-taking. This is a "how to think for yourself" technique.

Unit 2

IEW Unit 2 – Summarizing from Notes

Be sure they put the source document away and work only from their notes, the idea being that they should use their own words if possible and not copy from the original. However, if their paragraph ends up sounding very much like the original, do not fret; you are teaching a *process* at this point. Right now, they are imitating the writing process and structure. They will get more original and will find their own words, the more they practice. Remember to point out rules about indenting at the beginning of a paragraph, capitalizing at the beginning of a sentence and any proper nouns, and punctuating properly.

Work side by side with your students to model this process. Older students will become independent more quickly. Work with the students as long as they need help. You will know when they are ready for you to "back off" a bit. You are guiding them towards independence.

(TWSS Syllabus p. 10)

The exact directions in the Student Book (p. 5) are these:
1. **Handwrite** your rough draft.
2. **Indent** your first line.
3. **Capitalize** the first word of every sentence and any proper names.
4. **Double space** your paragraph. That means skip a line every time you start at the left side of your paper. So, you will leave a blank line every other time. Double spacing leaves room for editing, moving things around, and adding or taking out ideas, while leaving the paragraph moderately legible.
5. **Use pen**; not pencil. That way you will not waste time erasing. If you make a mistake, just draw one neat line through the mistake and keep going. Don't waste time scribbling it out or making a big blob of ink over it. (You might decide later that you want to revisit that idea. It would be helpful if it is still legible.)
6. **Your goals** here are
   - To look at your notes.
   - To think about the information.
   - To retell it in your own words and put those words on paper. You may add details that you remember as you go. You are not limited to just what you have in your notes. The notes are to *remind* you of the subject. Your paragraph should be 5–7 sentences.
   - To use the checklist from your teacher, or to make your own, and to check that you have included all requirements.

(TWSS Disc 1, *Scene Selection 2,* Unit II: Summarizing from Notes. View about 4 min. Syllabus pp. 9–14)

The student looks at one line in the outline and turns those key words into a sentence. Continue with each line from the outline until he has completed a rough draft.

Handwriting the paragraph (as opposed to typing) causes students to slow down and think about what they are writing. They should not hurry this process but ponder on what they want to say and choose their words thoughtfully. Younger students can do this through discussion while someone else scribes for them.

Style

As this process becomes familiar, begin to teach the dress-ups. Style is what will help make students' writing original and unique. The first stylistic technique you will introduce is the idea of being thoughtful about words they choose and not using bland words. We call these *banned words*, and they should try to avoid them. They are the boring, overused, dull, bland, and lifeless words. Talk to them about the Banned Words list on page 6 of the Student Book.

A fun project here is to get a big sheet of paper and help them make a Banned Words poster to put on the wall, or start a list they can keep in a notebook. Over time, you and your students can add new, alternative words to the poster as you come across them when you read aloud or do other activities. It will be an ever-growing list!

Each student is unique, progressing at his own pace. While new dress-ups will be introduced as you progress through the lessons, make sure only to require new dress-ups when the last one has become *easy*. With every paragraph, continue to require one of each dress-up that students have mastered, and add one new one (EZ+1). This will allow you to introduce dress-ups at the speed you deem necessary for each student. You will be able to tailor the same lesson for a younger student and for an older student, who will likely be able to go a bit faster.

EZ+1

Talk about choosing the best word for that particular thought or idea. Some words will work "ok" as alternates. A few words will seem really good. One word will be the *perfect* one. Have them look up some of the banned words and add more choices to the list on page 6 in their Student Book.

Make sure students have a thesaurus or synonym finder available, and show them how to use it. Consider having them highlight the word in the thesaurus when they look it up. Each time they flip through their thesaurus, they will see how often they have looked up alternative words.

- Students should read their paragraphs aloud.

By reading paragraphs out loud, students will often hear a mistake or something that sounds awkward, and they will correct it themselves, which is a skill that will serve them well.

- The student should hire an editor.

Talk to your student about finding someone to be his or her editor. Every great writer has an editor. Even great authors like Mark Twain and C.S. Lewis had editors who read over their work. The editor will simply read it and mark any glaring grammar infractions (that make it hard to understand), spelling, capitalization, and punctuation errors. They will make notations and hand it back. The student should look over the suggestions from the editor and consider the improvements. The editor can be you if there is no one else, but sometimes it is good to hear constructive criticism from a neutral party.

- Handwrite or type the final draft and illustrate.

When they are ready, either by hand or by typing they should revise the paragraph according to the input from their editor. It is fine if someone types it for them. Many students enjoy drawing an illustration to go with their paragraph.

- Review the checklist with your student, and be sure your expectations are clear.

At the back of the Student Book starting on page 147, your student will find all the checklists for each lesson. If they are new to IEW, then banned words will be the only thing on the style side of the checklist. If they are already familiar with IEW, they should be using all the stylistic techniques they have already learned.

EZ+1

TWSS Disc 2 teaches all the basic dress-ups. However, you will not teach them all at once! You will teach one dress-up at a time until that one becomes easy. Then teach the next one. The order the dress-ups are taught does not matter so much as the fact that you keep moving forward with the Units. Syllabus pp. 15–26.

 Younger Siblings: If you have younger siblings listening in, and you want them to have more practice with making key word outlines, find short, interesting paragraphs in something else they are reading. Be sure to choose short paragraphs (about one sentence for every grade level) that are *at or below* their reading level. They do not need to write a paragraph for each KWO. They can just create the outline, tell it back, and then go on to another one. Get them to a place where note-taking and telling back is familiar and easy for them, but do not linger too long in Units 1 and 2. About six weeks or so for younger students is plenty.

Analyzing Words

Located at the back of the Student Book (p. 131) and the Teacher's Manual (p. 67) is a list of words from the three books in *The Chronicles of Narnia* that your student is reading. There is an in-depth study guide sheet for each word. If you prefer that the students get through more words more quickly, you also have the option of having the students make their own vocabulary flash cards instead.

Either way, instruct the students to look up the word, find it in the chapter, and write down Lewis's sentence on their word analysis sheet or onto a 3 x 5 card with the definition. The section on analyzing words is optional; it will not be detrimental to the writing lessons if the activities are not completed. You will need to make copies of the blank analysis sheets. You may choose to have your student complete just the first page, or to complete both pages. There are instructions starting on page 66 of this Teacher's Manual. The words do not necessarily correspond to the lessons. The section is there for you to utilize as you wish.

Here are the next two paragraphs and examples of *possible* key word outlines.
(The Student Book only has an example of paragraph 1, Sherlock Holmes KWO.)

 Paragraph 2 – Illustrator – Sidney Padget

Illustrator – Sidney Padget

The main illustrator of the Sherlock Holmes stories was Sidney Padget. He got the job by mistake when the publisher addressed a letter of request for drawings to Sidney rather than to his younger brother Walter, who was a well-known artist. Over the years, Sidney drew hundreds of pictures for the Sherlock Holmes stories. When he began to imagine what Sherlock Holmes might look like, he used his brother Walter as the inspiration. There were other illustrators, but Padget was the first to draw Holmes with the long Inverness coat, the close-fitting cloth cap, and the pipe. That famous combination drawn by Sidney Padget is recognized all over the world as the character of Sherlock Holmes.

Sample Key Word Outline

   I. main, illustrator, Sidney Padget

   1. mistake, publisher, Walter

   2. SP, ✏ 100s, pictures

   3. brother, Walter, inspiration

   4. SP, 1st, ✏ coat, 🪈 cap,

   5. famous, combo, world, SH

The Student Book has a separate checklist for each of these three paragraphs.

Paragraph 3 – Sir Arthur Conan Doyle

Sir Arthur Conan Doyle

Sir Arthur Conan Doyle wrote many things, but he is most remembered for the fifty-six short stories and four novels about the detective Sherlock Holmes and his friend, Dr. Watson. Doyle wanted people to notice and read his other writings too, so he felt he had to put an end to the Holmes character. Doyle's readers loved the stories, and when he killed off Holmes in the story, "The Adventure of the Final Problem," which was published in 1893, his fans were extremely upset. Later, a publisher convinced Doyle to bring Holmes back because even though it had been about ten years, he was still a very popular character. "The Adventure of the Empty House" was published, and in it Doyle explains that Holmes had to fake his death to fool the evil Moriarty. The story was a huge success. Doyle died in 1930, and even though he wrote other works, he is most remembered for his Sherlock Holmes stories.

Sample Key Word Outline

I. Sir Arthur Conan Doyle,   stories,   SH,   Dr. W

    1.   SACD,   ppl,   notice,   writings

    2.   "The Adventure of the Final Problem,"   kills,   Holmes

    3.   publisher,   Holmes,   alive

    4.   "The Adventure of the Empty House,"   fake,   Moriarty

    5.   huge,   success

    6.   Doyle,   d. 1930,   remembered,   4,   SH

This course gives you two options for checklists.

1. The Student Book has checklists for each lesson with stylistic techniques preprinted on them.

2. The Teacher's Manual has optional, customizable checklists organized by IEW Unit rather than connected to a certain lesson. This way you can use them with any assignments beyond this course in the future. If you choose to use the Unit checklists, make a copy and keep the master clean. Review what your expectations are with the students. After a few times, you should have them add to a checklist with just a quick review from you.

Checklist by lesson

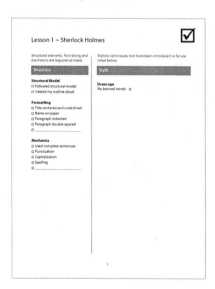

Customizable checklist by IEW unit

The Student Book already has a checklist to go with each lesson, so there are no copies to make. Every stylistic technique that is introduced will begin to accumulate on the checklists.

If it becomes too much for a particular student, cross off one or two until the first ones have become easy.

Each IEW unit adds more to the **Structural** side, so be sure to copy the correct unit's checklist. Some units may have more than one checklist depending on the number of paragraphs required.

The **Style** side can be filled in by the students with your direction, based on what stylistic techniques they already know and find easy to do, plus one they are learning to use.

"When you begin teaching the stylistic techniques, the preferred method is to teach all six dress-ups first. Then teach sentence openers after."

Teacher Notes: Lesson 2

Structure: IEW Units 1 and 2 – Key Word Outlining and Summarizing from Notes
Style: quality adjectives
Topic: Atlantis
Student Reading Assignment: Chapters 2–4

The goals of this lesson:
- To take notes from a source using the key word outline technique.
- To transfer the key words into complete sentences in paragraph form.
- To use a dress-up called the quality adjective.

Model the key word outline again on the board, encouraging the students to give you most of the key words. In order for the students to discover for themselves the importance of choosing good key words, they must be allowed to make some *not-so-good* choices at first. Allow the students to learn through the process. For example, if they choose a word poorly during the key word outline process, they will discover it when they test the outline aloud. Suggest that they go back, check the source, and adjust their outline. Before they begin writing the paragraph, review the checklist, so they know what is expected.

Here is the source paragraph from the Student Book:

Atlantis

Plato was a Greek philosopher who wrote about a great island city called Atlantis. Poseidon, the mythological Greek god of the sea, divided up an island into ten portions for his ten sons to rule. King Atlas, Poseidon's oldest son, was given the best section of the island, while the nine brothers, who were the nine princes of Atlantis, split up the rest. The island itself was round like a bull's-eye and had mountains, meadows, rivers, and high cliffs, which dropped off to the ocean. Seaports, bridges, cities, and palaces dotted the island. The Atlantean people were very well educated, wealthy, and had advanced technology. Plato tells us that the Atlanteans eventually became greedy for more wealth and treasures, and as punishment for their greed, the sea swallowed up the island of Atlantis, and it disappeared overnight.

Style

Assist students in completing Brainstorming Quality Adjectives (Student Book p. 13). Put some of the nouns on the board, and help them think of some quality adjectives that they might choose from. Require that they use at least one in their paragraph. Show them how to indicate the dress-up on their paper by underlining one quality adjective they have used. They may have used more than one, but they only need to underline one. Then they can put *QA* in the right-hand margin next to the line that contains the quality adjective. Review the checklist with the students before they begin.

Teacher Notes: Lesson 3

Structure: IEW Unit 3 – Story Sequence Chart
Style: strong verbs, -ly words
Topic: Jadis Tells a Story
Student Reading Assignment: Chapter 5

The goals of this lesson are for the students
- To identify the components of a story and their sequence.
- To make an outline based on the story sequence.
- To summarize a story from their outlines.
- To understand that each paragraph has a purpose.
- To use two new dress-ups.
- To create a clever title.

Characters and Setting, Plot and Conflict, Climax and Resolution

The source text for this assignment is from *The Magician's Nephew*, Chapter 5: The Deplorable Word. About two-thirds of the way through the chapter, Jadis begins to tell the story. Look for the paragraph that begins with, "It was my sister's fault." Read this paragraph and the next two, to gather your information about what happened. Stop three paragraphs down where Jadis ends with, "A moment later, I was the only living thing beneath the sun." Model the key word outline on the board, encouraging the students to give you most of the key words. This time the student is answering specific questions to identify story components.

Draw the chart from the next page onto the board just like Andrew does on the DVD. Complete all three outlines together at that time. Model for them how to use the questions to get the information.

While you model the KWO on the board, be sure and explain that they are welcome to put their own key words on their papers. After everyone has an outline, they should tell it back aloud and then begin writing their 3-paragraph story. They are to summarize the story and tell it from Jadis's point of view, just like in the book. When they reach the third paragraph, have them end with a *story clincher*, and show them how to pull 2–3 words from the story clincher to come up with a unique title.

Style
Starting on page 17 in the Student Book, there are some dress-up activities. You may always choose to do the activities before or after the outline. Give them some nouns to start with. Also have the students think of their senses when coming up with descriptions. How do things look, smell, feel, etc.

Q. How is Unit 3 different from Unit 2?

A. In Unit 2 the students take notes from a source, sentence by sentence. In Unit 3, they now get the key words by asking themselves questions. They then identify the components of a story in a sequence and write down key words for that component.

It is important to *outline* all three sections in one sitting, so the students can see the components. **This also introduces the idea that when you write, each paragraph should have a purpose.**

(TWSS Disc 2, *Scene Selection 3*, Unit III: Summarizing Narrative Stories. View about 30 min. until Andrew brainstorms for verbs. Syllabus pp. 29–36)

Story Sequence Chart for Narrative Stories

Characters/Setting

I. Who, When, Where?

Who is in the story?

What are they like?

Where do they live?

Where do they go?

When does it happen?

I.

  1.

  2.

  3.

Plot/Conflict

II. What is the problem?

What do they need or want?

What do they think?

What do they say?

What do they do? Feel?

II.

  1.

  2.

  3.

Climax/Resolution

III. Climactic moment (What moment
had you at the edge of your seat?)

Resolution (How is the problem solved?)

How is the need met/not met?

What happens after?

What lesson was learned?

III.

  1.

  2.

  3.

Story Clincher:

Story Clincher = Title

Remember:
The goal of Unit 3 is not to teach them how to write a story.
-Teach them to ask themselves questions.
-Teach them the components and sequence of a story. The end result is that they will be able to identify these components. When they decide to write an original story, they will know what to include and how to plan.
-Teach them that paragraphs have a purpose.

When creating a key word outline for a narrative story, do not choose words from each sentence. Choose key words that answer the questions for each paragraph's "theme."

Teacher Notes: Lesson 4

Structure: IEW Unit 3 – Story Sequence Chart
Style: Review quality adjectives (QA), strong verbs (SV), and -ly words.
Topic: Sister Tells a Story
Student Reading Assignment: Chapter 6

The goals of this lesson:
- To identify the story components and their sequence in a narrative story.
- To make outlines based on the Story Sequence Chart.
- To summarize stories from their outlines and consequently internalize the components of a well-constructed story.

Draw the chart, and model the key word outline on the board.

Once again, discuss the literary terms for each paragraph in the sequence: Characters and Setting, Plot and Conflict, Climax and Resolution.

This time the student will outline and summarize the same sequence of events, but instead of Jadis telling the story, the student will write *as if her sister is telling the story*. Instruct students to give the sister a name if they haven't already.

Style

Remind them to underline one of each dress-up per paragraph. Have them write the abbreviation for each in the right-hand margin so you can easily see that they attempted each one.
There is a list of -ly words on page 25 of the Student Book for them to use, and also on page 141. (When a new list of words is given in a lesson, an identical list is also provided in the back for convenience.) Point out the imposter list in the corner, and play the "pen test":

the _____ pen

If a word fits, it is an adjective. If not, it is probably an adverb. So, just because it is spelled with an *ly* on the end, doesn't automatically mean it is an -ly adverb. There are a few imposters!

(TWSS Disc 3, *Scene Selection 1,* Sentence Openers: "ly." View about 2 min. Syllabus pp. 15–21)

Assign the Analyzing Words assignment as time allows. You or the student may choose which words to study. There is no schedule so that you can decide the pace and the order.

Teacher Notes: Lessons 5–8

Structure: IEW Unit 4 – Summarizing a Reference
Style: In Lesson 6 you will introduce the *because clause* and *www.asia*.
Topics: London, Buckingham Palace, Parliament, and Westminster Palace
Student Reading Assignment: Chapters 7–8

The goals of these lessons:
- To take notes from a longer source.
- To limit their note-taking.
- To introduce the topic and clincher sentences.
- To write a concise paragraph that stays focused.

Point out to the students that this source paragraph is longer than the previous ones. Students must now take notes *from facts*, not from every sentence. The paragraph is longer, so there is too much information. For example, the source document on London has ten sentences with too much detail. The student needs to pluck out some facts and leave the rest. *This is more difficult to do than it sounds, and it is a very important skill.* Most students will need to work on this skill over a few paragraphs. Do several on the board together, and continue to model as much as they need.

Topic/Clincher Sentences
When they begin the key word outline this time, *leave the top line empty*. They should begin with the numbered lines; stop them at number 5. **The first and last lines will now serve a new purpose.** Teach the student that a paragraph should be an individual *unit of thought*, a single topic. The writer needs to introduce the reader to the topic of the paragraph. So the Roman numeral I will now house key words for the *topic sentence* of the paragraph. This is a general statement that simply introduces the topic. Teach the student to take his notes first, and then he will be more clearly able to see his topic and which key words to use for his topic sentence. The *clincher sentence* lets the reader know that the author is done telling about this particular topic. It clinches the idea! This should now be required on every paragraph except when writing narrative stories. **(TWSS Disc 3, *Scene Selection 2*,**

"The topic sentence and the clincher sentence must repeat or reflect 2–3 key words."

Unit IV: Summarizing a Reference. View about 12 min. Also *Scene Selection 2*, Writing Reports: Topic/Clincher. View about 2 min.)
Each lesson has a new source paragraph to practice with. Students should practice outlining and then write a concise paragraph with a topic and clincher that repeat or reflect 2–3 key words (reflect = synonym).

Style
In Lesson 6 you will introduce them to two new dress-ups: the *because* clause and www.asia clausal starters. The because clause is a unique thinking tool! It requires them to think of a reason for something. Go around the room and have each student finish a sentence that you start, using a because clause.

Have the student complete the activities, or do them together as a class, so they can utilize them in the next lessons. Both of these dress-ups will help them add more detail. Review the checklist with them.

Source texts from the Student Book for Lessons 5–8 are on the following page.

Lesson 5 – London

London has a long and rich history with the first record dating back to A.D. 43, when the city of Londinium was established by the Romans. In 842 Vikings attacked the city, and all was in chaos until Alfred the Great defeated the Vikings in 878. However, the Vikings came back, and in 1013 they ruled London again before being kicked out by Edward the Confessor. When Edward died, his nephew William, who was a Norman, took over the throne in 1066. There were many kings ruling in London over the years with many revolts and wars. In 1348, the Black Death swept through and killed one out of every three Europeans. Finally in 1800, London found itself the biggest city in the world. During the Second World War, London suffered terrible damage. Children from all over England were evacuated to the countryside to avoid all the bombing that was being done to the city. Today London is a well-established city of intrigue.

Lesson 6 – Parliament

Parliament is a part of the United Kingdom's system of government, called a constitutional monarchy. There are basically three parts: the queen, the prime minister, and the Parliament. The queen does not have much power or influence; however, she is the head of state. The prime minister proposes new legislation. Parliament has the power to enact real changes in laws and practice. Parliament consists of the House of Commons, whose members are voted in by the citizens, and the House of Lords, whose members are appointed by the queen. They meet at the Palace of Westminster to debate and decide on laws. Collectively, the House of Commons and the House of Lords are referred to as Parliament.

Lesson 7 – The Palace of Westminster

The Palace of Westminster itself has an interesting history. After William the Conqueror became King of England in the Battle of Hastings in 1066, his son, William Rufus, eventually came to reign in 1087. He wanted a new palace that was bigger than anything in England. The entire project was not completed, but a very big hall was finished. Over the next three hundred years, more buildings were added, and the palace was growing. By the 14th century it was in need of some repair and improvements. The two rows of pillars that held up the roof of the hall were taken out, and the old roof was replaced with a beautiful hammer-beam construction roof. Then in 1834, a fire nearly destroyed the entire palace. Among the buildings that survived the fire was Westminster Hall. A competition for a new design brought Sir Charles Barry in to head up the new structure. They were able to use all the buildings that made it through the fire, and the new palace was completed in 1870.

Lesson 8 – Buckingham Palace

Buckingham Palace is where the current royal family lives. The royal families have lived in Buckingham Palace since 1837. Architect Edward Blore built the original house in 1705 for the Duke of Buckingham. Later in 1761, King George III purchased the townhouse for his wife, Queen Charlotte. He commissioned an architect to expand the house. King George III died before it was finished, and his son King George IV also wanted to make it bigger, but he, too, died before it was finished. Finally, three weeks after she became queen in the summer of 1837, Queen Victoria was the first to actually live in it. The palace has 775 rooms, including 78 bathrooms. Currently, Queen Elizabeth and her husband, Prince Philip, Duke of Edinburgh, live there with other members of the royal family. However, it is more than just living quarters. There are many different rooms in the palace, which have many uses including offices, huge reception areas, banquet halls, and an enormous ballroom. In the mid-1800s, Queen Victoria requested that portraits of her immediate family be hung by the grand staircase, and they have not been moved in over 150 years. Visitors can view many of the rooms and enjoy the large art collection that is displayed in Buckingham Palace.

Teacher Notes: Lesson 9

Structure: IEW Unit 5 – Writing from Pictures
Style: review
Topic: How the Lamp-Post Came to Be
Student Reading Assignment: Chapter 9

The goals of this lesson:
- To observe and ask questions and write a paragraph of "event description." (This is not the same as the Story Sequence Chart from Unit 3.)
- To reinforce the topic-clincher relationship.
- To introduce the idea of asking quality questions of themselves to come up with content.
- To exercise imagination and creativity.

To begin outlining, students merely look at the picture and write down what they see. They should not add in or assume any other information other than what is observed in the picture. This observation is called the *central fact*, and these key words will be the topic sentence. They go on the first line with the Roman numeral.

Assist them if necessary to fill out the other lines with details that *they get to make up* by asking questions. Who is in the picture? Where are they? What are they doing? What is going on outside the picture? What else is in the picture?

The topic sentence and the clincher sentence should be written in **past tense**; they tell about the central fact of the picture. The details students fill in should be written as a flashback. Think of it as the past within the past, like a remembrance of details that happened even earlier than the event in the picture. This is called the *past perfect tense*, and writers use the helping verb *had* with the main verb to convey that they are talking about another time before the past.

> **Simple Example:**
>
> I. Topic sentence (central fact): Beautiful Jadis threw the iron bar towards Aslan.
>
> 1. Detail: She **had been** the queen of a great nation.
>
> 2. Detail: The citizens of Charn **had** always **treated** her with great reverence.
>
> 3. Detail: Never **had** anyone **spoken** to her in such a way.
>
> Clincher (central fact): In frustration, Jadis threw the iron bar at the Great Lion.

Notice the clincher is repeating words from the topic sentence.

(TWSS Disc 4, *Scene Selection 1*, Unit V: Writing from Pictures. View about 25 min. until Andrew asks about sources for Unit 5. Syllabus pp. 47–52)

Be sure to review Lesson 9 in the Student Book before you begin teaching this lesson.

Lesson 9 ~ A Lamp-Post Is Planted

At the end of Lesson 9 in the Student Book, there are three optional pictures from *The Lion, the Witch and the Wardrobe* (LWW). Even if your students have not read LWW before, they can still observe what is in the picture, ask themselves questions, and make up what the picture is about. The paragraphs do not have to be true to the Narnia stories. Students can make up the details as the questions are answered. They simply describe what they see and answer questions to make up the rest.

There is also an example of how you could apply Unit 5 – Writing from Pictures to other studies. (See Student Book p. 40.) The example paragraph is written as if the students have just read about Marie Curie in a history book and may now have images of her life in their minds. The paragraph is written as though Marie Curie is telling about her memories.

Assign the Analyzing Words assignment as time allows.

Teacher Notes: Lesson 10

Structure: IEW Unit 6 – Fused Outlines and Library Research Reports
Style: review
Topic: Primrose, Buttercups, Daisies
Student Reading Assignment: Chapters 10–12

The goals of this lesson:
- To take notes from a longer source such as a library book, which requires students to take *notes from facts*, not from each sentence.
- To take notes from multiple sources and then rewrite those notes into one *fused outline*, from which they will write their own paragraph.
- To make decisions on what information to leave out as they limit their notes to a specific focus.

Unit 6 is similar to Unit 4 because there is a lot of information, and the student will have to decide what to include in his notes and what to leave out. However, with Unit 4 there was just the one source document, whereas Unit 6 has multiple source documents. Unit 6 teaches students that they can have multiple source documents (or library books). They will take notes from each, which they will "fuse" into one <u>logically ordered</u> outline with a topic and clincher.

Read the student instructions with your students.
This lesson has three separate parts for the *purpose of practicing the fusing*; the source documents are short and simple. Have them practice on all three flower topics in this lesson. Take a day for each flower.

"Give short, frequent assignments."

Start with the primrose paragraphs. Each paragraph has a blank outline next to it. Students will take their notes from facts, not necessarily from each sentence. These are just general notes that they think are interesting or important about the topic of the primrose flower. They will not have a topic and clincher just yet.

After they have done all three outlines from the three primrose paragraphs, they will combine, or fuse, those notes into a new single outline, using the blank outline (Student Book p. 43). They will have to leave out some information they originally took notes on. (See TWSS Syllabus p. 44.) After they fuse the information, they will come up with a topic and clincher on the fused outline, and then they are ready to tell back and write their paragraph. There is a sample composition in the back of this Teacher's Manual on pages 96–97.

The main goal is to *practice the fusing* technique.
(TWSS Disc 5, *Scene Selection 1*, Unit VI: Library Research Reports. View about 20.5 min. until Andrew comments about sources. Syllabus pp. 37–44)

When they get to Lesson 11, they will need a *thorough* understanding of this process, as the sources are much longer and more complex.

From Student Book p. 42

The Bold and the Beautiful

The primrose flower is a gorgeous flower with vivid colors, unlike other springtime bloomers which are usually of lighter pastels. It seems to boldly demand attention with yellows, blues, and reds. Some of the colorful primrose can be found flourishing as far north as Canada and Greenland. They are also found all over England, as their striking colors dot the landscape.

Poisonous Primrose

The primrose makes a lovely addition to a shady garden, and it also likes the rocky areas. The beautiful petals usually stand about ten inches off the ground on slender stems. However, the innocent primrose has a dark side that few know about: It is poisonous to cats. Cats may be able to sense this, but pet owners should not plant any flower belonging to the primrose family in their gardens.

Flower Facts

There are over three hundred fifty species in the primrose family. The cowslip is the only one that smells like black licorice. The loosestrife blossom loves damp, swampy areas and will bloom all summer long. Some of the primrose that grow in America are not very attractive, but the English primrose is ravishing. The name *primrose* comes from the Latin word, *primis*, which means *first*, and primrose means *first love*.

From Student Book p. 44

The Lovely Buttercup

The delicate and lovely yellow flowers that bloom each spring are a favorite of many. The sunny blossoms, which are about the size of a quarter, grow just about anywhere. The buttercup is part of the *Ranunculus* genus, which means *little frog*. The brilliant yellow flower grows in over 36 distinct types just in North America. It can stand up to 24 inches high and sometimes has hairy stems.

Buttercups Are Not for Dinner

Many wild plants can be eaten for survival or just to spice up a recipe. However, the buttercup is not one of them. The buttercup belongs to the *Ranunculus* genus, which has over 600 species. Every plant from this group will have some very nasty effects when eaten fresh by grazing animals. It leaves a very acidic taste in their mouth, which the animals do not like. Unfortunately if a field is overgrazed, the animals will resort to eating the buttercups resulting in blisters, excessive saliva, and abdominal pain. Hay with buttercups in it is safe for animals to eat because the buttercups are dried out, and the poison is broken down.

Buttercups

Some children are told that butter comes from cows that have eaten a buttercup flower. This is not true, of course, just as chocolate milk does not come from cows that have eaten a chocolate bar. The buttercup is often associated with *childishness* because of its simple and delicate design. Most buttercups have five buttery-yellow petals, and down in the very center is a tiny amount of nectar for a determined insect to find.

From Student Book p. 46

Daisies

Daisies are sweet and simple and are often associated with innocence and love. During Medieval times a maiden would make a garland of daisies that she would wear in her hair to let a gentleman know she was saying yes to his proposal of marriage. Many girls would pick a flower, pull off one petal at a time, and say, "He loves me; he loves me not," until she was down to the last petal, and then she would know the truth of his feelings. This silly ritual began with daisies in the Victorian age and is still practiced today.

Daisies in Literature

Famous authors such as Shakespeare, Chaucer, and Dickens wrote about daisies in many of their literary works. Only the rose and the lily are written about more. When he was dying, author John Keats said that he could already feel the daisies growing up on his grave. The saying "pushing up daisies" is a term used regarding death or being close to it and may have been started by the author's comment.

The Daisy Cure

Long ago people learned to use plants and herbs for healing. They would mix daisy flowers with water and then treat a bruise on someone's leg or arm. It later became known as bruisewort. It was also used to try to cure insanity. Because the daisy looks like an eye, it was thought that it could cure eye problems. People thought warts could be removed with the power of the daisy, and they also thought it would keep you from growing.

Teacher Notes: Lesson 11

Structure: IEW Unit 6 – Fused Outlines and Library Research Reports
Style: who/which clause
Topic: The Crown Jewels of England
Student Reading Assignment: Chapters 13–15 (Finish the book.)

The goals of this lesson:
- To take notes from a longer source such as a library book, requiring students to take notes from facts, not each sentence.
- To practice combining, or *fusing*, all their notes into one outline.
- To teach a new dress-up: the who/which clause
- To generate a bibliography.

This lesson is very similar to Lesson 10 with the flower paragraphs; only now the paragraphs are longer, more detailed, and more complex. Students will still need some guidance to limit information they take notes on.

Usually when researching a subject, your students gather a few library books that have some information on their subject. It is also helpful to consult an encyclopedia for topic ideas. Right now let's look at how students would utilize their library books. In this lesson, source texts are given so that students can practice the note-taking more quickly.

Each source is talking about an aspect of The Crown Jewels of England Collection, but each source has a different focus. Point this out to the students, and talk to them about narrowing their focus too. After all, one could write volumes about the subject of the crown jewels. Their assignment is to write one paragraph of five to seven sentences on one topic, such as the history, the gems themselves, or the items in the collection, within the bigger subject.

Read the student instructions with your students. Talk to the students about narrowing the topic down. There is a lot of information. Have them read all three sources to get a feel for what is being said in each before they decide on their focus topic.

(TWSS Disc 5, *Scene Selection 1*, Creating a Fused Outline. View about 4 min. Syllabus pp. 37–44)
Students will need a blank sheet of paper, or they can use the prepared fusing outline in the Student Book on page 55. There is a copy of the fusing sheet in this Teacher's Manual on page 28 as well. This sheet will allow them to put all of their notes onto one page. The sheet has a small stylistic checklist as a reminder, and it does include more stylistic techniques than have been taught in this course as of yet. Cross off what they have not been introduced to yet, but keep a master copy for future assignments.

See TWSS Syllabus p. 40, Unit 6 Teaching Procedure: Stage Five.

As you prepare, you may wish to do your own KWO on these paragraphs and fuse them, in order to become familiar with the information and appreciate this process.

Style
When students begin to write a paragraph, they might recall more detail. How to add it in without having too many sentences can be a dilemma. Show them how to add some detail with a *who/which* clause. *Who* is used to add detail about a person, and *which* is used to add detail about a place, thing, or idea. So, you can explain that these are like big long adjectives. Usually, commas enclose a who/which clause. Students will indicate usage by underlining the <u>who</u> or the <u>which</u>, and writing *w/w* in the right-hand margin.

(TWSS Disc 2, *Scene Selection 1*, Dress-ups: who/which. View about 10 min. Syllabus p. 18)

Make a column on the board with nouns (and modifiers) from their paragraphs. Then help them brainstorm.

A sword,	<u>which</u> was brilliantly inlaid with dazzling colored jewels,
The crown,	<u>which</u> was only used at the most sacred and special occasions,
Queen Elizabeth,	<u>who</u> was so distraught when her husband died,
King Peter the Cruel,	<u>who</u> was a greedy and terrible ruler,
The sceptre,	<u>which</u> _____
Edward the Confessor's sapphire,	<u>which</u> _____
The coronation,	<u>which</u> _____

Bibliography
The students are now researching and taking facts from multiple sources, and they should keep track of their sources and provide a bibliography at the end of their paper. This is only a one-paragraph assignment, but it is good to introduce the skill of keeping track of their sources. When they get to a bigger essay or report, the bibliography will not be a new concept. After they have gathered the information, they should list the sources alphabetically by author's last name. Fictitious information is provided for them to use. They need to write down the following information about each printed source they use:

- author's name
- title of the publication (and the title of the article if it's a magazine or encyclopedia)
- date of publication
- the place of publication of a book
- the publishing company of a book
- the volume number of a magazine or printed encyclopedia
- the page number(s)

Source 1

Crowns

The origin of the use of a crown is not known. A crown or headpiece of some kind has been used in many cultures from many parts of the world as long as records have been kept. The crown is used to denote the majesty or royalty of someone. The person who was heir to the throne or who had taken control of a throne or a group of people wore a circlet, a headdress, or crown of some kind. A crown was usually decorated with jewels, gems, precious metals, or other items of significance from that culture. When not being worn at some special occasion, the crown was kept in a safe place and guarded.

The Crown Jewels of England is an exquisite collection of many beautiful things that includes the crowns that the kings and queens of England wear. The collection is under guard at the Tower of London. It includes three glorious crowns, each with a rich and interesting history, as many of the diamonds, rubies and other gems have been acquired or handed down from one king to another. One of the crowns in the collection was crafted for Queen Elizabeth, the Queen Mother. It has a diamond called the Mountain of Light diamond. Another crown, the Imperial Crown of State, has a diamond called the Second Star of Africa. Besides the huge diamond, this crown has over 2000 other diamonds, 277 pearls, along with sapphires, emeralds, and rubies. The third crown in the collection is called the Imperial Crown of India and has over 6000 diamonds and other jewels.

Scott, Jeremy. *Crown Jewels.* King George, Virginia: Diego Publishing, 2010. 10–11.

Source 2

Dramatic Histories

Many of the precious stones mounted on items in The Crown Jewels of England Collection have a story behind them. For instance, Edward the Confessor had a ring that contained a beautiful blue sapphire. When he died in 1066, he was buried with his crown and with his sapphire ring. Approximately 200 years later, an elaborate tomb was built by King Henry III for Edward the Confessor's body. They opened the coffin and decided to remove the crown and the ring. This beautiful sapphire now sits atop the Imperial State Crown.

Another gem, a blood-red ruby, has had many owners. King Peter the Cruel murdered another king after luring him to a dinner and then took the ruby from him. He later gave the ruby to Edward the Black Prince as a thank-you gift. Later Edward's son Richard had the ruby with him when he was captured by Henry IV in 1399. Richard was murdered, and Henry illegally took the throne and the ruby. Henry's son, Henry V, wore a battle crown with the ruby mounted in the center. The large ruby later turned up on the crown of Richard III in 1485. When he was killed in battle, the ruby dislodged from the crown and was lost as it rolled under a bush. It was later found by Lord Stanley and given to Henry Tudor. The 5-centimeter ruby traded owners a few more times before being mounted into the Crown of State.

A third jewel, a diamond called the Mountain of Light, is on the crown that was made for Queen Elizabeth, the Queen Mother. This huge diamond comes with a blessing and a curse. It is said that any woman who has it will have good luck, and any man who has it will meet with disaster. Over the years, many of the men who have had it in their possession have met gruesome deaths. The Queen Mother, however, lived to the age of 101. The stories behind the jewels continue to fascinate!

James, Kyle. *Tales of the Crown Jewels.* Fredericksburg, Virginia: James Publishing House. 2010. 43.

Source 3

Swords and Scepters of the Crown Jewels of England

There are five swords and two scepters in The Crown Jewels Collection. One sword in particular is called the Jeweled Sword of Offering, which has diamonds, emeralds, and rubies. The gems are arranged to represent the Thistle of Scotland, the Shamrock of Ireland, and the Rose of England. The Jeweled Sword of Offering is the most valuable sword in the collection. The largest sword is called the Sword of State. The other three swords are the Sword of Temporal Justice, the Sword of Spiritual Justice, and the Sword of Mercy. It is believed that these exact swords were made for the coronation of Charles I of England. A coronation is the formal ceremony that occurs when there is a new king or queen. The scepters are also used in the coronation. The Scepter with the Cross and the Scepter with the Dove were both made in 1661. However in 1905, the Scepter with the Cross was refitted with the largest diamond in the world called the Great Star of Africa. The Scepter with the Dove has several bands of jewels on it and an enameled dove on top, which symbolizes the spiritual authority of the monarch. Both scepters are held, one in each hand, as the new king or queen is crowned.

Michael, Joseph. *Scepters and Swords of Europe.* New York: Dutton. 2011. 87–90.

itle resource #1 _____

. _____
. _____
. _____
. _____
. _____
. _____
. _____

Title resource #2 _____

1. _____
2. _____
3. _____
4. _____
5. _____
6. _____

Title resource #3 _____

1. _____
2. _____
3. _____
4. _____
5. _____
6. _____

TOPIC:

Topic Sentence Key Words:

← repeat or reflect 2-3 key words →

1. _____
2. _____
3. _____
4. _____
5. _____
6. _____
7. _____

Clincher Sentence Key Words: _____

Fused Key Word Outline

My personal checklist:

◇ Strong Verb
◇ Quality Adjective
◇ Because clause
◇ www.asia clause
◇ who/which clause
◇ -ly word
◇ #2 prepositional opener
◇ #3 -ly word opener
◇ #4 -ing opener
◇ #5 clausal opener
◇ #6 VSS
◇ Decoration _____

EZ+1

Cross-off the dress-ups you have not learned or found to be easy yet.
Always include the ones you find easy plus one more.

The Lion, the Witch and the Wardrobe

Lesson	Writing Topic		Chapter for Reading Assignment
12	Air Raids	31	1
13	Evacuations from London	35	
14	The White Witch	37	2–4
15	The White Witch	37	5–8
16	The White Witch	37	9–11
17	The White Witch	37	12–14
18	Adolf Hitler	41	15
19	Roosevelt and Churchill	43	16
20	C.S. Lewis	45	17
21	The White Witch and Hitler	47	
22	Churchill and Roosevelt	51	
23	Churchill and Lewis	53	

Teacher Notes: Lesson 12

Structure: IEW Unit 4
Style: triple extensions
Topic: Air Raid on London during WWII
Student Reading Assignment: *The Lion, the Witch and the Wardrobe*, Chapter 1

The goals of this lesson:
- To take notes from a longer source. (Stage One – See p. 33 for an extended outline of the stages.)
- To practice *limiting* in note-taking.
- To compose topic and clincher sentences.
- To write one concise paragraph that stays focused on one topic.
- To teach a new stylistic technique: Sentence Styles–Triple extensions (TWSS p. 23).

In this lesson, students will work on a paragraph about World War II—specifically about the air raids on London by the Germans, who were led by Adolf Hitler. Model for them, and work with them to complete a key word outline. Take notes from facts, not from each sentence. Take some; leave the rest. Read the entire paragraph aloud together before you begin.

After the KWO is completed, have students tell back the KWO in complete sentences.
Before they begin writing their paragraph, discuss the triple extension examples from Winston Churchill. Help them brainstorm some triple extensions of their own, and then encourage them to pick one and weave it into their paragraph.

Style
On page 17 of the TWSS, you will a variety of triples: triple words (QA, SV, -ly, etc.), triple phrases, triple clauses. On page 60 of the Student Book are many famous quotes using triples (and more) from Churchill. As demonstrated in the Churchill quotes, there are many ways to utilize these triple extensions. Some are more effective than others. The quotation people remember most from Churchill was probably:

> "Never in the field of human conflict was <u>so much</u> owed by <u>so many</u> to <u>so few</u>."

It is short and to the point and not overdone. Think of things in threes; then try putting them in a series, and then work them neatly into a sentence. For example, they could repeat the *same word, the same part of speech, or the same ending on words, phrases or even clauses.* Keep the grammar construction parallel. Some wipe-off board suggestions are on the next page.

(TWSS Disc 3, *Scene Selection* 2, Summarizing a Reference. View about 10 min. until Andrew mentions 500-word paragraphs. Syllabus p. 37)
(TWSS Disc 4, *Scene Selection* 3, Stylistic Techniques: Decorations & Triple Extensions. View until Andrew begins listing decorations. Also, *Scene Selection* 4, Triple Extensions. View about 5.5 min. Syllabus p. 23)

Assign the Analyzing Words assignment as time allows.

Lesson 12 ~ Air Raids

After discussing the Churchill quotes with your students, draw columns on the board, and help them brainstorm how they might incorporate a triple extension into their next composition.

Ask them questions to get them thinking:
- What are some of the things (nouns) military forces use?
- Can you think of three adjectives to describe one of those nouns?

As they answer, fill in the grid on your wipe off board. Inspire them by putting up some of your own ideas too. Have them choose or circle the three they like the best.

bombs	tanks	soldiers	planes		
destructive	armored	ruthless	merciless		
explosive	fortified	heartless	countless		
aggressive	unstoppable	mindless	endless		
pulverizing	impregnable	dissolute	relentless		
targeting	thundering	nefarious	fearless		
macerating	rumbling	vicious	deafening		
devastating	booming	malicious	thundering		
unfaltering					

Try to pick three that have the same ending (-ive, -less, -ed, -ing).

You can also make lists with verbs and -ly words to go with them.
- What three things could you say about how St. Paul's Cathedral was standing that next morning? Describe how the cathedral stood in the aftermath. *Stood* is a verb, so use three -ly words (adverbs) to modify how the cathedral stood, e.g., *desperately, defiantly, determinedly, bravely, stubbornly, angrily, triumphantly, wearily.*

- How were the firefighters working to save the city? Use three -ly words (adverbs) to describe their actions, e.g., *unfalteringly, tirelessly, courageously.*

- Churchill was *valiant, resilient, resolute* … (More advanced students might try using a metaphor or simile to compare St. Paul's Cathedral to Churchill.)

After all of the ideas are up on the board or on their papers, have them choose one to put into their paragraph.

Teacher Notes Regarding Units 4 and 6

If you will refer to your TWSS Syllabus starting on page 37, there are levels or *stages* within Unit 4 and 6 that you should be aware of. Different assignments will use one of these stages within the body paragraphs of a report. Familiarize yourself with each stage, and view the appropriate TWSS DVD to see how Andrew Pudewa demonstrates each one.

Unit 4 Teaching Procedure:

Stage One: Outline and summarize one topic from a one-paragraph source. The skill of limiting begins here. Students must choose three to five details to put in their outline and leave the rest.

Stage Two: Outline and summarize one topic from a multi-paragraph source. Allow four to six details. It is helpful to read the entire source first, so they know what is available before they start choosing. They will summarize in one paragraph.

Stage Three: Outline and summarize two or more topics from one source. The length of this source varies depending on the levels of the students.

Unit 6 Teaching Procedure:
This is where Unit 4 blends into Unit 6. (See TWSS Syllabus pp. 40–41.)

Stage Four: Outline one topic from multiple sources. Students will produce one outline on the topic from each source. If there are three sources, they will have three outlines for the same topic. Students combine some of the facts from the outlines into one *fused* outline, and then from the fused outline they write one paragraph.

Stage Five: Outline multiple topics from multiple sources. Each source may cover the same topics and multiple topics. They will outline each topic from each source on its own outline and then fuse. They will do this for all three topics they have chosen. When they have fused each topic down to one outline, they will summarize each topic into a paragraph.

"If you teach the how-to of research with shorter and more frequent one-, two-, and three-paragraph compositions, students will naturally understand how to approach a longer and more detailed research project when they are required to do so."

Source Text from Student Book p. 59

German Air Raids

When Hitler, leader of Germany, decided he would try to dominate the entire world, he started by attacking countries that were nearby. Poland, Austria, and France were among the first. After France was beaten down by the German army in June of 1940, England became the next target in Hitler's sight. Winston Churchill, who was the British prime minister, knew what was coming, and in a speech right before the bombings started, he warned his citizens that the Battle of Britain was about to begin. By September of 1940, "The Blitz" had begun, and the air raids did not cease until June of 1941. The Germans bombed heavily, and there were fires all over the city of London. Brave firefighters dodged debris as they sped about the city putting out as many fires as possible. Many buildings, churches, factories, and homes were saved by these courageous men. St. Paul's Cathedral was not touched by the fires or the bombings, and it stood while fires and destruction surrounded it on all sides. Churchill would not surrender or negotiate with Hitler, even though other countries had done so. His Navy and fighter pilots kept up defense of the small island. When it was all over, Churchill said of the pilots, "Never in the field of human conflict was so much owed by so many to so few." Hitler's plan of world domination had definitely been derailed by Churchill and the brave people of England.

Teacher Notes: Lesson 13

Structure: Combination of IEW Units 3, 4, 6, 7
Style: dress-ups that appeal to the five senses
Topic: Evacuations from London
Student Reading Assignment: Chapter 2

The goals of this lesson:
- To practice limiting in note-taking.
- To identify and plan out the components of their journal story.
- To compose historical fiction.

The end result of this lesson is for students to write four journal entries about their experiences as evacuees from London. They will fuse key words from facts and made-up key words into historical fiction journal entries.

1. Read the paragraph aloud, and help them pull out some facts they can use in the observations as children in this setting. They won't be able to take notes on everything in all three paragraphs. They will have to leave out some details. **(Unit 4)** The source text from their Student Book is also on page 36 in this Teacher's Manual.

2. The brainstorming activity on the next page will help students flesh out some details *as if they were there*. They should not answer with silly or nondescript answers. This is not an "ad-lib," fill-in-the-blank, funny exercise. Here they must use the technique of asking themselves questions to find information in their brains. **(Unit 7)**

> Example: What food do you pack? They should not answer with *snacks*. They should answer with a realistic, detailed list of foods, such as *cheese, hard-boiled eggs, apples, salt pork, and bread*. Help them as much as they need.

3. Then help students *fuse* the information from both of the activities above into journal entries **(Unit 6)**. They may also include any details from the paragraph from Lesson 12 if they wish. Model how to write from the *first person perspective*. They will not fuse into an outline like before; rather they will *mentally fuse* as they write.

As I packed my journal, mom brought me a bundle of cheese, bread, and dried meat to take on the train.

4. Before students begin writing, review the components of a story from the Story Sequence Chart **(Unit 3)**, so they can think about and plan out their components.

They can make up a fictional name for themselves, change their age and number of siblings, etc. That part is all made up. When you review the components of a good story from the Story Sequence Chart (Unit 3), point out that there must be conflict, or it will be boring. Students will not follow the Story Sequence Chart itself, however. The chart is just to get them thinking about the components in their mind as they go along. Put the names of the components on the board, but not the chart. Just remind them of the vocabulary of the components of a good story.

As they use the facts from the key word outline of the factual paragraph and some of the made-up answers to make journal entries, they should write *as if they were really living through this time*. On their next page they will handwrite the entries. Help them think about the dates of the entries.

- The first entry is the day they find out, and they go home to pack.
- The next entry will be while they are traveling on the train or ship.
- The third entry is when they arrive at their new, temporary home.
- The fourth entry will be for the day they get to return home.

These dates will not be four days *in a row*. The first three might be closer together, but then the last one should be a year or so later. They may choose to write more than four entries, so they can include events in between, but they must *include* these four particular points in time in their final finished draft. Let them be creative. They may decide that their character does not even return from the temporary home. This is historical fiction, so they really have some freedom here within the context of the situation. Review the lesson in the Student Book thoroughly before teaching.

Assign the Analyzing Words assignment as time allows. Challenge them to use one of the words they have analyzed in their paragraphs.

Source Text from Student Book p. 64

Evacuations: Air Raids Are Expected

In September of 1939, the evacuations began. Hundreds and thousands of children would be sent to the countryside. Teachers sent home notes telling the parents what to pack, such as a gas mask, clothing, soap, food, and maybe a small toy or favorite book. Some children were parted from their parents for the first time, as they went to school that next morning knowing they would not return for a long time. Once they arrived at school, the children were loaded onto a bus, which them took them to points north of London. Notes pinned to the children told their name, what school they were from, and where they were to be delivered.

By 1941, almost 1.5 million children had been evacuated. Some ended up in good homes, while others were starving and ate their toothpaste or glue just to survive. Many children were able to send letters home and communicate with their parents. Most of the children went to school while they were away. Some children enjoyed life in the country, and some saw real cows for the first time. Many of the children did not believe that milk came from cows, while others did not want to eat carrots that someone pulled from the ground, insisting that they only ate carrots from a can.

Not all of the children went to the English countryside. Some children went as far as America or Canada and were gone for a long time. Some children never made it back home. Their information was lost, and some died of sickness or starvation. However, most of them did return to be with their families when the war was over, never forgetting the scary and lonely experience.

Units 4, 7

Teacher Notes: Lessons 14–17

Structure: IEW Units 4 and 7
Style: dress-up: www.asia and decoration – the dramatic opener
Topic: The White Witch
Student Reading Assignment: Chapters 2–14

The goals for these lessons are for the student
- To take notes from a multi-paragraph source (**Unit 4, Stage Two** [see p. 33]).
- To write a concise paragraph that stays focused on its topic.
- To be introduced to character analysis.
- To learn the job of a conclusion and introduction in a five-paragraph composition (**Unit 7**).
- To be introduced to the concept of a thesis statement.

In Lessons 14–17, students will write a five-paragraph essay. The teacher notes are combined for these lessons. With Lessons 14–16 they will create the body paragraphs. In Lesson 17 they will learn how to create the conclusion and then the introduction. As always, review the lessons in the Student Book, so you can plan out how and when you will introduce and teach each lesson; help your students become aware of the parts of an essay and how they relate and work together. The students have a checklist for each lesson in their book.

Style
In Lesson 14 you will also teach the www.asia adverbial clausal starter. Review the Student Book, and put the same example sentence on the board for them to finish using each of the www.asia clausal starter.

Lessons 14–16
Body Paragraphs
The students are to look in *The Lion, the Witch and the Wardrobe* for their facts. The Student Book tells them which chapters to refer to, and there are questions on the side of their outline to guide them. The students are looking for clues as to the Witch's character and the things she did that demonstrate different character traits.

Each paragraph should convey proof (facts) about a different character trait. They may need to look at the list of character traits provided or perhaps brainstorm more to choose from. Review each lesson, and help them decide on what character trait they see. When they look for clues within the book, have them take notes on the provided outline. Offer guidance when they try to figure out her motives.

Lesson 17
Conclusion and Introduction Paragraphs
**(TWSS Disc 5, *Scene Selection 2*, Introduction & Conclusion. View about 5 min.
Syllabus pp. 53–58)**
The Student Book gives an outline structure to follow, including the Decoration: Dramatic Opener for the introduction paragraph.

The next page suggests some discussion questions, or *prompts*, to help students think about the White Witch. They may also choose a Bible reference for each of the three character traits. Introduce the idea of a *thesis statement*—a concept that may be new to some—which they must understand as they enter the upper middle school age and beyond. Talk about it, and then *help them write it.*

When they are finished, they will have a five-paragraph essay about the White Witch. This is not retelling the story; within the novel they are looking for facts about the White Witch. If they are allowed, instruct them to underline phrases or make notations in their book as they read.

Example questions, or prompts, to use while introducing the concept of a thesis statement:
- What effect did the White Witch want to have on everyone? How did she accomplish this?
- What was the ultimate goal of the White Witch?
- Did the White Witch feel more powerful after causing other people to suffer?
- Do greed and power ruin people?

You may choose to have them use a Bible verse in each of the body paragraphs:
- Romans 8:5 ~ Those who live according to the sinful nature have their minds set on what that nature desires.
- Proverbs 21:10 ~ The wicked man craves evil; his neighbor gets no mercy from him.
- Proverbs 28:28 ~ When the wicked rise to power, people go into hiding; but when the wicked perish, the righteous thrive.
- Isaiah 5:20a ~ Woe to those who call evil good and good evil.
- Proverbs 26:24 ~ A malicious man disguises himself with his lips, but in his heart he harbors deceit.
- Psalms 10:2 ~ In his arrogance the wicked man hunts down the weak, who are caught in the schemes he devises.
- Romans 16:18 ~ By smooth talk and flattery, they deceive the minds of naïve people.
- Jeremiah 9:8b ~ With his mouth each speaks cordially to his neighbor, but in his heart he sets a trap for him.

Have them look up some verses of their own; these are just examples. They may also use quotes from famous leaders if you prefer.

Each of the three body paragraphs is following the White Witch through the story, so her motives are different at each part. At first she is trying to trick Edmund, so Jeremiah 9:8b goes nicely there.

Her motives and actions change throughout, and so each of the three paragraphs might have a different focus on the character traits she shows. The conclusion and introduction will bring it all together with the thesis *that you will help them come up with or even write for them.*

Use this to discuss the reading and what they take notes on. Let them give their thoughts and opinions. This is an introductory assignment that will be a good stepping-stone to other more difficult assignments as they move forward. The next page has a list of some character traits.

Character Traits

bold / fearful
diligent / lazy
enthusiastic
forgiving
generous
gentle / harsh
joyful / sad
just / unfair
loyal
thoughtful
obedient
patient / impatient
responsible
truthful / untruthful
determined
displeased
aggressive
proud
bitter
peaceable
sweet
brutal
heroic
spiteful
vengeful
deceptive
thankful
poetic
arrogant
haughty
resentful
hospitable
soft-spoken
innocent
domineering
narcissistic
gracious
tyrannical
intelligent
clever

"Give them the vocabulary so they can think the thought."

If you are using the Unit checklists, make a copy of the Units 7/8 checklist that is for five paragraphs. Otherwise, they have a checklist for each lesson at the back of their book.

When you teach the conclusion and introduction paragraphs, point out that they do not need all the dress-ups and openers in these two. They should choose two or three dress-ups and then vary the openers, but it is not necessary to use *all* of them.

Also, the body paragraphs will tend to be roughly the same size, while the conclusion and introduction may very well be slightly smaller. This is fine.

Assign the Analyzing Words assignment as time allows.

Teacher Notes: Lesson 18

Structure: IEW Unit 4
Style: #2 and #3 sentence openers
Topic: Hitler
Student Reading Assignment: Chapter 15

The goals of this lesson are
- To take notes from a multi-paragraph source (Stage Two).
- To practice limiting in the note-taking process.
- To write a concise paragraph that stays focused.
- To learn different ways of beginning a sentence to vary the patterns.

Students should look in the provided source text for their facts. (A copy of the source text is on page 42.) This is a short assignment, but they will use what they learn about Hitler in a future essay where they will compare and contrast him with the White Witch. Short, frequent assignments give them needed practice.

If this assignment is easy for your student, go ahead and assign Lesson 19 as well. They will KWO and write similar-sized paragraphs on Roosevelt and Churchill. Note that there is another dress-up to teach along with a decoration in Lesson 19.

"Give short, frequent assignments."

Style

With this lesson you will teach the second and third sentence openers. The #1 sentence opener is the Subject opener. This is what is commonly used and we want to encourage the students to veer away from always starting their sentences the same. The #2 opener is the preposition and the #3 opener is the -ly word.

There is an activity in the Student Book, which you may want to replicate on the board or have the students participate orally until they know how to do it.

When they label their papers, they will simply encircle the *2* or *3* in the left-hand margin next to each sentence. You may also choose to have them label all of their #1 subject openers too. As they learn more openers, it helps to see how many subject openers they are still employing. The goal is not to have more than two in a row of any opener, which they will until they learn the other openers.

Source Text from the Student Book page 77:

Upon becoming chancellor of Germany, Hitler made changes immediately. He made a new law called the Enabling Act that would give him emergency powers for four years. He also took away all freedoms from the German citizens. German police could walk into any house without a warrant to search or arrest without cause. He had other political rivals murdered, so no one could oppose his new laws.

Looking to the future, he ensured that every German would go along with anything he planned, by changing some of the educational material the government schools were using. He had the curriculum in the schools updated to include Nazi education, including a morning salutation of "Heil Hitler."

He set up a secret police force called the Gestapo, who spied on everyone. Anyone caught saying anything against the Nazi Party or Hitler would be arrested. The secret police also kept a close eye on the Jews, whom Hitler had hated for a long time. They were kept from holding prominent jobs and going to school. Within six years, most of the Jews had either been arrested and killed, were in hiding, or had fled the country.

By 1933, he had taken complete control of Germany. He was *der Führer* (German for: "the Leader").

In 1939, in a bold move that only took days, Germany invaded and conquered Poland, and World War II had begun. It did not take long before the German army was at England's doorstep.

Sources:

Daynes

Grant

Teacher Notes: Lessons 19

Structure: IEW Unit 4
Style: #6 sentence opener and decoration 3SSS
Topic: Roosevelt and Churchill
Student Reading Assignment: Chapters 16

The goals of this lesson are
- To take notes from a multi-paragraph source (Stage Two).
- To practice limiting in the note-taking process.
- To write a concise paragraph that stays focused.
- To learn another way to begin a sentence to vary the patterns.
- To learn a decoration using 3 Short Staccato Sentences

Students should look in the provided source text for their facts. (A copy of both of the source texts is on page 44.) This is another short assignment, but they will use what they learn about Roosevelt and Churchill in future essays. Short, frequent assignments give them needed practice.

Style
Review the Very Short Sentence activity from the Student Book page 81. Talk about the examples and see if the students can make up some as well. Five words or less makes a VSS. In the left-hand margin of their paper they will put a *6* and circle it.

Also on page 81 of the Student Book is a decoration activity. This one is easy. They just put three Very Short Sentences together. This is called 3SSS   Three Short Staccato Sentences. On page 23 of the TWSS there are some more examples. Review the sentences in the Student Book and see if the students can come up with some. This is a decoration, and the label for decorations would normally go in the right-hand margin, but in this case it affects the openers as well, so just have them put 3SSS in the left-hand margin.

Lesson 19 ~ Roosevelt and Churchill

Source Text from the Student Book page 79:

Franklin Delano Roosevelt, or FDR, was the American president at the time of Hitler's attempted take over of Europe. He was able to send money, supplies, and even ships to Britain, but the law prevented him from sending soldiers. FDR was a fiercely loyal and honorable man who would not back down when he knew he was in the right and did all he could to help his friends in England.

He got those traits from his loving mother, who often read to him as a boy before getting him a private tutor. His father took him sailing many weekends, but died when Franklin was just 18 years of age.

A determined student at Harvard, he was always interested in politics and was involved with the school government. This led to an exciting life in politics, including two terms as state senator and then as Assistant Secretary of the Navy. However, in 1921 he came down with polio and was paralyzed from the waist down. Not letting that stand in his way, he wore heavy leg braces and became the governor of New York and then president of the United States.

Congress had passed a law that stated America would not get involved in conflicts abroad unless attacked first. When Japan attacked Pearl Harbor, it stunned and enraged President Roosevelt and the American people. Now he could send troops and help out the tired British army and his friend Winston Churchill.

Source:

Faber

Source Text from the Student Book page 80:

As a boy Winston Churchill disliked school, except for English. He loved reading and writing and had an exceptional memory. His father was a politician in Britain's House of Commons, and when Winston visited his father and listened to the proceedings, he was fascinated. They were arguing fiercely, but he was amazed at the well-thought-out oratory from each speaker.

Winston decided he would join the army, and he loved the action, but there was a lot of spare time. While the other officers played cards, he studied, read, and wrote. He gathered books on government, history, and politics and became quite knowledgeable on each.

An opportunity came to be a war correspondent in India, and he went, hoping to see battle up close. On another similar trip to South Africa, the train jammed on the tracks, and the enemy captured them. In a daring escape he was able to find his way to an Englishman, who hid him for three days before loading him up with supplies and getting him to safety. He then wrote another book about his adventure in Africa.

Churchill was in France during World War I for a short period of time, and after the war ended, he and his wife moved to a house in the country. He continued to write while making repairs to the old manor, but he missed the action and excitement of politics.

When Hitler invaded Poland in 1939, Winston was invited to give radio updates on the war, and his upbeat and eloquent way with words was a boost to the morale of the British people. Soon after, Winston became the prime minister of England. As Hitler's army advanced closer to the little island, England was alone, and her future looked bleak. Churchill vowed that they would not buckle under the weight of Germany's forces as the other countries had done. At least, that was the hope.

Suddenly, Japan launched an attack on the Americans, and that actually gave Churchill what he needed! America had been sending supplies and ships, but no soldiers. Now Roosevelt was able to send troops as well. The war ended in 1945, and he was getting old. He kept writing and won the Nobel Prize for Literature in 1953.

Sources:

Dowswell

Daynes

Teacher Notes: Lesson 20

Structure: IEW Unit 4
Style: advanced dress-up: dual quality adjectives, strong verbs, -ly words
Topic: C.S. Lewis
Student Reading Assignment: Chapters 17

The goals of this lesson are
- To take notes from a multi-paragraph source (Stage Two).
- To practice limiting in the note-taking process.
- To write a concise paragraph that stays focused.
- To learn an advanced dress-up.

Students should look in the provided source text for their facts. (A copy of this source text is on page 46.) This is another short assignment, but they will use what they learn about Lewis in a future essay. Short, frequent assignments give them needed practice.

Style

The duals are easy to teach. They already know how to use quality adjectives, strong verbs, and -ly words. They will just double them up, using *and* or any other coordinating conjunction: *for, and, not, but, or, yet, so* (**fanboys**). See page 18 of the TWSS.

There are some examples in the Student Book to put on the board or work through orally.

Optional Research Assignment

This lesson has an optional assignment on page 85 of the Student Book. If you wish, the students should research how each of the three men they just wrote about used radio broadcasts to reach people before and during WWII.

This optional five-paragraph assignment will allow them to use the skills they have learned with regard to note-taking using key words, limiting their notes, and then summarizing their notes. If you assign this optional work, they will need access to the library and possibly the Internet, in which case, look ahead in this manual to page 47 as well, and pick up some books for Lessons 21–23 if you wish to assign extra research.

Source Text from the Student Book page 83:

Clive Staples Lewis announced at the age of four that he was to be known from now on as Jack. As he grew, Jack very much enjoyed school and especially enjoyed translating works from Latin to English. Norse myths were also a favorite. His tutor, Professor Kirkpatrick, taught Jack Greek, which also led to his learning French and Italian.

When he was at college in 1916, he knew he might be sent to the war, and he could have gone home to Ireland to wait it out, but he chose to stay and do his duty. At first he was briefly in charge of escorting new recruits to training, but he soon found himself in the trenches in France. He contracted a fever and spent a short stint in the hospital, where he continue to read and write. He returned to the front lines, and while leading his men toward the German line, friendly fire came too close. When he awoke, all of his friends had died. After his return to college, he had his first book published. It was a book of poems entitled *Spirits of Bondage*.

Back at school he continued to write, and the awards and honors were piling up. He was now busy with lecturing at the college along with other public speaking engagements. Later he and his friend J.R.R. Tolkien formed a literary group they called *The Inklings*. Everyone in the group was a writer, and they all critiqued and encouraged one another's work. They had fascinating discussions, and Lewis learned to use words very precisely.

Sources:

Benge

Grant

Teacher Notes: Lessons 21–23

Structure: IEW Unit 8

The goals of these lessons are for students

- To realize that there is more than one structural model for a longer essay (such as a compare/contrast essay).
- To organize their thoughts and information in a logical order.
- To experience a writing assignment that allows some creativity.

TWSS Disc 6 covers the formal essay and includes the persuasive essay model. Andrew Pudewa does not specifically go over compare and contrast essays in the TWSS, but you can see that the format of the introduction and conclusion are the same; in addition each body paragraph must be a concisely worded and organized *unit of thought* with a topic and clincher that repeat or reflect.

There are structural models to guide you. (The optional first model is the easiest, and while there is not a specific assignment for that model, feel free to use it if it better fits your students.)

For lessons 21–23 they will use their own essays from Lessons 14–20 as source material. Although you may wish to assign extra research time so they have extra notes to fuse together for these assignments. If you are able to make a trip to the library ahead of time, pick up some books that are at or below their reading level and not too long. They do not need a lot of information. The people they will be writing about are

> the White Witch (They should have enough on her.)
> Adolf Hitler
> Franklin Roosevelt
> Winston Churchill
> C.S. Lewis

The structural models for the next three lessons are shown together on the next page, so you can see the differences.

Notes about Lessons 21–23

There are different ways to *arrange* a compare and contrast essay, based on ability level of the writer and the purpose of the essay. As you look down the models, you can see that each one forces the student to come up with more details and examples for each idea, building into bigger and more complex paragraphs. Always put the structural model on the board, so the students can see the arrangement. The body paragraphs (BP) need to stay consistent in construction. If they start with the White Witch and then talk about Hitler, the other paragraphs need to follow that order too.

No lesson

```
I.    Introduction Paragraph

II.   BP    General info on White Witch

III.  BP    General info on Hitler

IV.   BP    Compare and Contrast
            one main idea

V.    Conclusion Paragraph
```

1. Five-Paragraph Model
Give general information about the first subject in one body paragraph (BP). Then give general information about the second subject in the second body paragraph. Then the third body paragraph will compare and contrast. This may be an easier option for a younger student to start with. The Student Book does not have a specific lesson to go with this model, but you could walk them through it if you choose.

Lesson 21

```
I.    Introduction Paragraph

II.   BP    White Witch and Hitler both …

III.  BP    WW and H was not …

IV.   Conclusion Paragraph
```

2. Four-Paragraph Model
Another good option for a younger student is to just have two body paragraphs. One for the similarities (no more than three), and one for the differences (no more than three).

Lesson 22

```
I.    Introduction Paragraph

II.   BP   Idea 1
           Churchill and Hitler were both …
           However, C was … and H was not.

III.  BP   Idea 2
           C and H were both …
           Although, C was …, H was not.

IV.   BP   Idea 3
           C and H were both …
           Yet, C was …, but H was not.

V.    Conclusion Paragraph
```

3. Five-Paragraph Model
Compare and contrast different ideas on each person, together in each of the three body paragraphs. All three body paragraphs should stay consistent with the order in which the ideas are introduced. Transitional words are especially helpful with this type of paragraph.

Lesson 23

```
I.    Introduction Paragraph

II.   BP Idea 1 Churchill
III.  BP Idea 1 Lewis

IV.   BP Idea 2 C
V.    BP Idea 2 L

VI.   BP Idea 3 C
VII.  BP Idea 3 L

VIII. Conclusion Paragraph
```

4. Eight-Paragraph Model
Each idea is encompassed in its own paragraph now. There is more room for more detail and examples. The first and second body paragraphs will also be on the first idea and how it applies to each person. Then the third and fourth body paragraphs will be on the second idea for each person. The fifth and sixth body paragraphs will be on the third idea for each person.

Teacher Notes: Lesson 21

Structure: IEW Unit 8
Style: nothing new
Topic: The White Witch and Hitler
Student Reading Assignment: Finish the book.

The goals of this lesson:
- To show one way to put together an essay that compares and contrasts two people.
- To write concise paragraphs.

Here is the basic structural model for this assignment:

```
Title
```

The thesis sentence and the clincher sentence in the conclusion paragraph will repeat or reflect the same idea.

The trick is that the thesis sentence will be at the end of the Introduction paragraph, and they will not write that paragraph until last.

So, after they have written out their body paragraphs and they start writing the conclusion paragraph, help them think about what they discovered or learned for themselves.

Assist them in turning that idea into a statement or declaration.
Then use that idea to craft a simple clincher sentence, and restate the idea in the thesis sentence from the introduction.

I. **Introduction**:
Attention getter
Background information
Brief statement about the similarities
Brief statement about the differences
Thesis: State what is going to be shown or proven. This will be repeated/reflected in the clincher.

II. Body paragraph about the **similarities**:
6-8 sentences with examples of 2–3 similarities
Topic and clincher sentences repeat or reflect.

III. Body paragraph about the **differences**:
6–8 sentences with examples of 2–3 differences
Topic and clincher sentences repeat or reflect.

IV. **Conclusion**:
Restate who you were comparing/contrasting.
State what was the most significant *similarity* between these two people.
State why you chose it to be the most significant.
If you choose, put a Bible verse here that is relevant.
The clincher should repeat or reflect 2–3 key words from the **thesis** (last sentence from your Introduction) and your **title**.

The Student Book contains a chart on page 87, which you may want to recreate on the board to better assist students with ideas. This chart will help them organize the similarities and differences the two people have. Assist them in filling out the chart. Try to come up with six to eight ideas for each column. They will choose the three strongest.

The Student Book guides them through forming the body paragraphs. The first body paragraph details the ways they are *same*. The second body paragraph details the ways they are the *different*. Finally, there are outlines for a conclusion paragraph and an introduction paragraph.

Again, help them with the thesis, even *if you write it for them*. This is a new and difficult concept. You are modeling how to do it. <u>You are exposing the student to a new idea, the thesis statement. They do not have to completely understand it now.</u> Similar to introducing and talking about the periodic table before actually getting to a real chemistry class, you are slowly introducing the idea now into their brains, so it can be pulled out again later. Do not panic if you are also unsure of the correct way it should be written. We are just introducing the *idea* and the *vocabulary*.

Throughout the entire process, be sure and have students read aloud what they have written so far. Is there too much repetition? Does it flow? Help them to see where they might improve. This is a different type of essay than what they might be used to. Do not worry about helping them too much. You cannot pull something out of their brains that is not there yet. Also, this analytical writing is hard for younger students. Help them as much as they need. Help them bounce back and forth between the thesis and clincher until they understand the purpose. You are modeling for them how to do this. When they are completely finished, have them read the paper aloud to someone who has not heard any of it yet. Listen to the feedback.

(TWSS Disc 6, *Scene Selection 1*, Write the Body Paragraphs First. View about 2 min. Syllabus p. 59)
The typical essay has five paragraphs. This assignment only requires four paragraphs, with the body paragraphs giving a lot of details and examples.

Note: Introduction and conclusion paragraphs will not have the usual requirement of all dress-ups and openers. Have them choose two or three dress-ups, and they should always vary the sentence openers. *As possible,* the body paragraphs should have each dress-up they know. Review the checklist with the students before they begin, so they understand what the requirements are.

Review the lesson in the Student Book before you begin. Also, look over the sample compositions from the back of this book to give you and your students ideas.

If you are using the customizable checklists, make a copy of the Unit 7/8 checklist, and review it with the students before they begin writing. Otherwise, the Student Book has a checklist for Lesson 21. Make sure your expectations clear.

Assign the Analyzing Words assignment as time allows.

Teacher Notes: Lesson 22

Structure: IEW Unit 8
Style: #5 clausal opener and the transitional opener
Topic: Churchill and Roosevelt
Student Reading Assignment: Finish the book.

The goals of this lesson:
- To experience another way to arrange an essay that compares and contrasts two subjects.
- To write concise paragraphs.
- To look at two new sentence openers.

Compare and contrast essays have a few structural models to choose from, so the students always have some flexibility when they write. In Lesson 22 the students will write another essay comparing and contrasting two people; only this time the arrangement will change.

The book does not provide another chart like the one in the Student Book, page 87. The idea is to give them the tool once (page 87) and then have them duplicate it themselves in subsequent assignments. Hopefully it will be a tool they use later as well. Have them draw the columns on a sheet of paper, similar to what they used on page 87 of the Student Book. Use their writing from Lesson 19 as their source, although they may wish to review the source text from that lesson, or even do some extra research to add in as well.

With this essay, they will think about the thesis before they begin and will write a rough draft thesis argument. (See Student Book page 93.) Remind students: A thesis should present an arguable idea. What opinion are they trying to prove? They should take a stand, state their opinion with authority, and then give all the reasons, examples, or evidence to back it up. This is, again, *exposing them to an idea*, exposing them to the vocabulary. Help them wrestle through it and write a good thesis.

Style

You will also teach the #5 clausal opener and the transitional opener. The Student Book has a practice activity for them to complete prior to the writing assignment. The activity is on page 94 of the Student Book. Model some examples on the board for them.

If you are using the customizable checklists, make a copy of the Unit 7/8 checklist, and review it with the students before they begin writing. Make your expectations clear.

Assign the Analyzing Words assignment as time allows.

Here is the basic structural model for this assignment:

The thesis sentence and the clincher sentence in the conclusion paragraph repeat or reflect the same idea.

The trick is that the thesis sentence comes at the end of the introduction paragraph, and they will not write that paragraph until last.

So, after they have written out their body paragraphs, and they start writing the conclusion paragraph, help them think about what they discovered or learned for themselves.

Assist them in turning that idea into a statement or declaration.
Then use that idea to craft a simple clincher sentence, and repeat the idea in the thesis sentence up in the introduction.

Title

I. **Introduction**:
Attention getter
Background information
Brief statement about similarities
Brief statement about differences
Thesis: State what is going to be shown or proven.

II. Body paragraph- Compare and contrast **Idea 1**.
4–6 sentences give details about idea 1.
Topic and clincher sentences repeat or reflect 2–3 **key words**.

III. Body paragraph- Compare and contrast **Idea 2**.
4–6 sentences give details about idea 2.
Topic and clincher sentences repeat or reflect 2–3 **key words**.

IV. Body paragraph- Compare and contrast **Idea 3**.
4–6 sentences give details about idea 3.
Topic and clincher sentences repeat or reflect 2–3 **key words**.

V. **Conclusion**:
Restate who you were comparing/contrasting.
State what was the most significant similarity or difference between these two people.
State why you chose that to be the most significant.
If you choose, put a Bible verse here that is relevant.
The clincher should repeat or reflect 2–3 key words from the **thesis** (last sentence from your introduction) and your **title**.

Review the Student Book before you begin, and model as much as possible on the board for the students. Discuss it with them. What are their thoughts and ideas? If possible, have willing students stand at the board with you, and work out ideas together.

Teacher Notes: Lesson 23

Structure: IEW Unit 8
Style: review
Topic: Churchill and Lewis
Student Reading Assignment: Finish the book.

The goals of this lesson:
- To show another way to arrange an essay that compares and contrasts.
- To write concise paragraphs.

The students will write another compare and contrast essay. This final structural model is the longest and gives the students more room to fill in the details and examples that they may have had to leave out with the other two structural models. This will be an eight-paragraph essay.

Discuss the arrangement with the students. If possible recreate the entire structural model on the board before class begins. This assignment may take them two weeks or more. If your schedule allows, give them the time they need to think through what they want to say and write the paper well.

Review the lesson in the Student Book, and model for them as much as possible. They will use the papers they wrote in Lessons 19 and 20. They may refer back to the original source documents for those lessons, and you may also choose to allow them to research on their own and fuse in more facts. Have them draw up the columns and brainstorm more ideas than they will need. Then choose the three strongest.

Be flexible with the assignments, and be sure to tailor the lessons to fit the levels, needs, and challenges of your students.

Be sure they review the checklist and turn it in with the paper.

Title

I. **Introduction**
Attention getter
Background information
State the **three ideas** to be compared and contrasted.
Give your **thesis** statement.

1st idea or point

II. **Idea 1** as it pertains to Churchill
Give three examples and details.
Should be around 6–8 sentences with a
topic and clincher that repeat or reflect

III. **Idea 1** as it pertains to C.S. Lewis
Give three examples and details.
Should be around 6–8 sentences with a
topic and clincher that repeat or reflect

2nd idea or point

IV. **Idea 2** as it pertains to C
Give three examples and details.
Should be around 6–8 sentences with a
topic and clincher that repeat or reflect

V. **Idea 2** as it pertains to L
Give three examples and details.
Should be around 6–8 sentences with a
topic and clincher that repeat or reflect

3rd idea or point

VI. **Idea 3** as it pertains to C
Give three examples and details.
Should be around 6–8 sentences with a
topic and clincher that repeat or reflect

VII. **Idea 3** as it pertains to L
Give three examples and details.
Should be around 6–8 sentences with a
topic and clincher that repeat or reflect

VIII. **Conclusion**
Restate who the two people are.
State what was the most significant similarity or difference **between them.**
Why did you choose it? Defend your conclusion.
Restate key words from your **thesis** in your clincher, and **those key words**
should also reflect in your **title.**

Lesson	Writing Topic		Chapter for Reading Assignment
24	Chores	57	1
25	*The Lion, the Witch and the Wardrobe*	59	
26	Shasta	61	2
27	Bree	61	3
28	Aravis	61	4
29	Aslan	61	5–6
30	The Horse, His Boy, and Aravis	63	7–9
31	*The Horse and His Boy*	63	10–15

Teacher Notes: Lesson 24

Structure: IEW Unit 7
Style: review
Topic: Chores
Student Reading Assignment: *The Horse and His Boy*, Chapter 1

The goals of this lesson:
- To take notes from the brain.
- To practice thinking in threes (three themes or three related topics).
- To compose topic and clincher sentences.
- To write concise paragraphs that stay focused.

In this lesson, the students write on something they know about, *chores*. They will choose and organize their information and write a five-paragraph essay. Below and on p. 58 are some brainstorming ideas about chores that you can put on the board. Hopefully, the students will have many ideas to add. Review the Student Book before you begin.

Topic Ideas:

Kinds of chores
Frequency of chores
Difficulty of chores
Training for chores
Feeling of satisfaction when completed
Extra chores
Chore chart for organization
Helping siblings with their chores

Could any of these be broken down into three smaller topics?

Kinds: kitchen duties, bathroom duties, doggie duties, etc.
Frequency: daily, weekly, monthly, etc.
Difficulty: easy/quick, harder/takes longer, very difficult

After they brainstorm many ideas about chores, have them choose just three of the ideas.
These will be the topics of the three paragraphs.
Here are some examples:

Topic 1	kinds
Topic 2	frequency
Topic 3	feeling of satisfaction after finishing

Topic 1	kitchen duties
Topic 2	bathroom duties
Topic 3	bedroom duties

Topic 1	easy/quick chores
Topic 2	harder chores that take longer
Topic 3	difficult chores I'm still mastering

Replicate student page 110 on the wipe-off board. Be sure to include the questions from the right-hand side of their page.

After they choose three topics, have them begin to ask themselves questions to fill in the outlines. Then they will write three body paragraphs, each with a topic and clincher that repeat or reflect.

Students will outline and write the conclusion. Then they will outline and write the introduction. Blank outlines are provided in the Student Book. Model on the board.

(TWSS Disc 5, *Scene Selection 2*, Unit VII: Creative Writing. View about 13 min. Stop when Andrew mentions the Aristotelian Model. Syllabus p. 53)

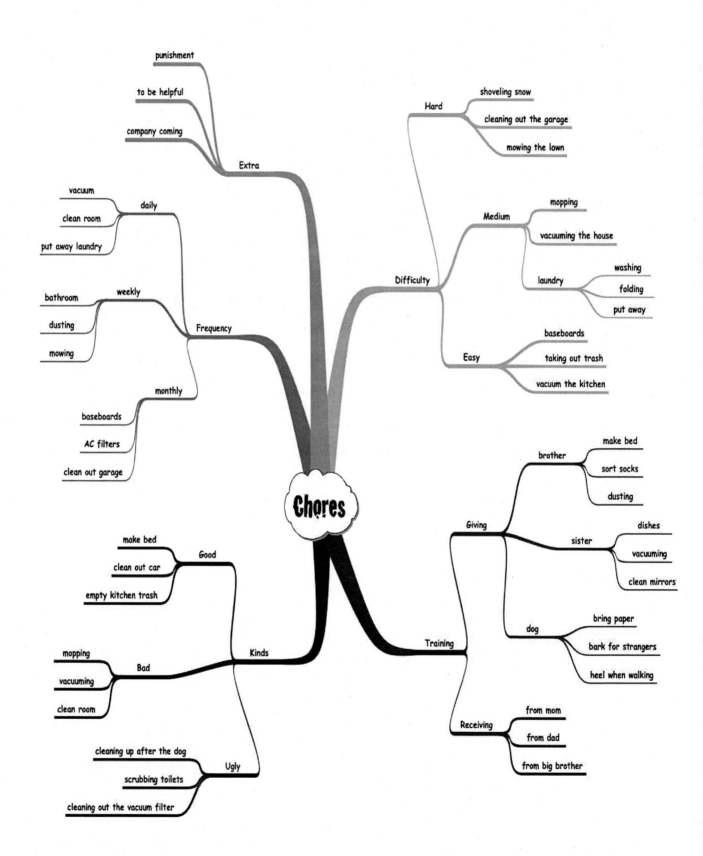

Teacher Notes: Lesson 25

Structure: IEW Unit 9
Style: review
Topic: *The Lion, the Witch and the Wardrobe* (LWW)
Student Reading Assignment: Refer back to *The Lion, the Witch and the Wardrobe.*

The goals of this lesson:
- To practice using the Unit 3 Story Sequence Chart.
- To put the Story Sequence Chart into a five-paragraph essay to write a different form of the traditional book report—a critique.

In this lesson, students write a five-paragraph composition called a *critique*. They will summarize the story in the body paragraphs of the essay and simply add conclusion and introduction paragraphs.

Model the Story Sequence Chart on the board, and walk through LWW. An example is provided below. Your students may offer different answers. Guide them, and use as many of their answers as possible. The key is not to get too detailed. Each of these three paragraphs should be five to seven sentences, and they will *not* have topic and clincher sentences.

The Lion, the Witch and the Wardrobe

Who are the main <u>characters</u>?
(There are too many to name everyone.)
What are they like?
Where are they?
<u>Set the stage</u>…

I. Pevensie children, 3-good, innocent 1-selfish
   1. Witch, evil, cruel
   2. Aslan, loving, protector
   3. Narnia, magical, winter, ~~Christmas~~

<u>Plot</u>? What is going on?
What is the <u>problem</u>?
What do they do?

II. White Witch, rules, land
   1. WW, tricks, Ed, bring others
   2. children/army, prepare, fight
   3. WW, deep magic, Ed→ treason

<u>Climax</u>?
<u>Resolution</u>?

III. Aslan, sacrifices, himself
   1. stone table, splits, Aslan alive!
   2. Aslan, defeats, White Witch
   3. children, rule, Narnia, years

After you and the students fill out the Story Sequence Chart, they should write three paragraphs to summarize the story. Then they will outline a conclusion and finally the introduction. There are structural model outlines in the Student Book. Make a copy of the Unit 9 Critique checklist, or have them pull it out of the back of the Student Book, and review it with them before they begin.

Assign the Analyzing Words assignment as time allows.
(TWSS Disc 6, *Scene Selection 2*, Unit IX: Critiques. View about 21 min. Stop when Andrew ends discussion of Unit IX. Syllabus pp. 67–71)

Lesson 25 ~ Critique of *The Lion, the Witch and the Wardrobe*

Teacher Notes: Lessons 26–28

Structure: Response to Literature
Style: review
Topic: Character Analysis of Shasta, Bree, and Aravis
Student Reading Assignment: Chapters 2–4

The goals of these lessons:
- To realize that when thinking about literature, the key skill is the ability to ask oneself questions and answer them.
- To begin to develop a literary vocabulary.

Each of these three lessons directs the student in creating a key word outline by answering some questions about a character. They may refer back to the story to get details or examples as needed. These paragraphs should have a topic and clincher that repeat or reflect. <u>Review the Student Book before you begin.</u>

Shasta is a shy, agreeable person, whereas Bree and Aravis have stronger, more robust personalities. Your students may need help to figure out what they think about each character. The outline questions are there to guide the student. Literature should evoke responses from the reader, so each student may see something different as they read the story. Be flexible.

Style
There are no new stylistic techniques in these lessons. They should just continue to practice the ones they know and find easy. Help them brainstorm dress-ups on the board before they begin. How could we describe Shasta's clothing? How could we describe his living conditions? If they have not mastered all of the stylistic techniques covered in this book, continue to add one *when they are ready*. If they ever struggle with any of the dress-ups, it may be an indication that they have not found them all to be easy. Work with them, and find out which ones are easy and which ones they have trouble with.

Teacher Notes: Lesson 29

Structure: Response to Literature
Style: review
Topic: Symbolism Analysis
Student Reading Assignment: Chapters 5–6

The goals of these lessons:
- To continue asking and answering questions about something specific.
- To memorize the structure to use with future assignments.
- To realize that they may have questions of their own.
- To further develop their literary vocabulary.

When using these structural models, note that they are meant to be flexible so that the student can pull these models and utilize them with any story. Feel free to create a different model. Change the questions. Ask the students if they have any questions that they think would be good to use. Plug those in. Review the Student Book, and make a copy of the Units 4, 5, 6 checklist for them.

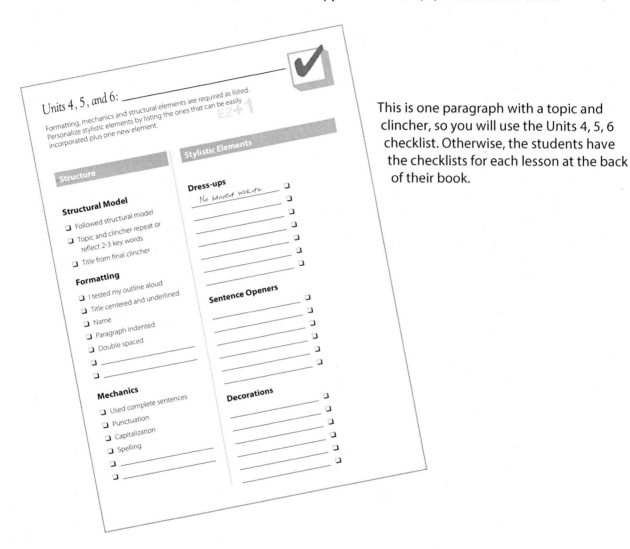

Units 4, 5, and 6: _____
Formatting, mechanics and structural elements are required as listed.
Personalize stylistic elements by listing the ones that can be easily incorporated plus one new element.

EZ+1

Structure

Structural Model
- ❏ Followed structural model
- ❏ Topic and clincher repeat or reflect 2-3 key words
- ❏ Title from final clincher

Formatting
- ❏ I tested my outline aloud
- ❏ Title centered and underlined
- ❏ Name
- ❏ Paragraph indented
- ❏ Double spaced
- ❏ _____
- ❏ _____

Mechanics
- ❏ Used complete sentences
- ❏ Punctuation
- ❏ Capitalization
- ❏ Spelling
- ❏ _____
- ❏ _____

Stylistic Elements

Dress-ups
No banned words

Sentence Openers

Decorations

This is one paragraph with a topic and clincher, so you will use the Units 4, 5, 6 checklist. Otherwise, the students have the checklists for each lesson at the back of their book.

Continue to assign the Analyzing Words assignment as time allows. Encourage students to use these words in their own writing.

Response to Literature Lessons
Taken from the 2010 Writing Educator's Symposium

Teacher Notes: Lesson 30

Structure: Response to Literature
Style: review
Topic: Theme Analysis
Student Reading Assignment: Chapters 7–9

The goals of these lessons:
- To continue asking more focused questions.
- To develop students' understanding of literary vocabulary.

Help them see that stories have themes, and that one theme in this story is the idea of *pride*. There may be more than one theme. As the students have been reading, maybe the ideas of *friendship* or *loyalty* jump out at them. That is great. Literature should evoke responses from the reader. They may be able to relate to the friendships in the story because of something they have experienced. Perfect! Encourage them to write about what they come up with!

Students should use the outline to help them organize their responses into a logical order. They will write one paragraph with a topic and clincher. They may need to come back to this paragraph after they complete the entire book and see if they want to change or add anything once that they know the outcome.

Review the lesson in the Student Book before you begin.

Teacher Notes: Lesson 31

Structure: Response to Literature
Style: review
Topic: Response to *The Horse and His Boy*
Student Reading Assignment: Finish the book.

The goals of these lessons:
- To learn an alternative structure for critiques or book reports.
- To continue learning literary vocabulary.

With this final lesson, students will choose two of their previous analysis paragraphs and add them to three new paragraphs they will write, to put together a five-paragraph essay as a response to the book, *The Horse and His Boy*. Review the lesson from the Student Book before you begin. The three new paragraphs they will write will be

- a one-paragraph summary of the story (Unit 3~Story Sequence Chart)
- a conclusion
- an introduction

Response to Literature Lessons
Taken from the 2010 Writing Educator's Symposium

There are structural models in the Student Book to assist them with the organization of their thoughts, ideas, and answers.

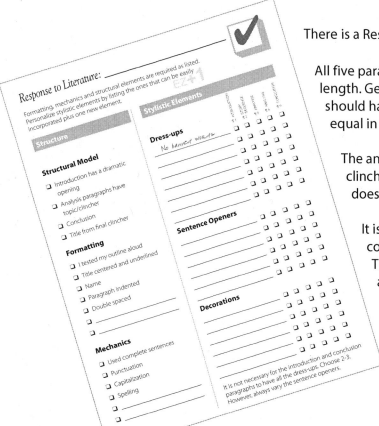

There is a Response to Literature checklist on page 87.

All five paragraphs do not need to be of equal length. Generally, the three body paragraphs should have the most information and be more equal in length.

The analysis paragraphs have a topic and clincher, while the story sequence paragraph does not.

It is not required that the introduction and conclusion have all the stylistic techniques. They may choose two or three dress-ups and vary the sentence openers.

Analyzing Words

"Give them the vocabulary
so they can think the thought!"
—Andrew Pudewa

Analyzing Words

There are different ways to approach a study of vocabulary words. Your goals and objectives should be taken in to account when you begin.

- If memorization of many words with quick, short definitions is the goal, then making flashcards for word study would be a good choice. Write the word on one side of an index card, and have the students look up and write the definition on the back. Illustrations and an example sentence can also aid in memory.

- If a more thorough knowledge of words at a more thoughtful pace is the goal, then doing a more in-depth word analysis would be a good choice. This section includes the word analysis pages for the students. A younger student might only complete the first page of the word analysis, while an older student may be able to complete both pages. Either way, do the first word analysis with the students, so you know they understand, and you will know how long it might take them on their own. The students will not always find something to go in every section. That is ok.

If you choose to have your students complete the word studies, it is *not* mandatory that they do all the words, nor is it necessary that they do them *along with* the writing lesson. It is fine if the writing lesson and the vocabulary words do not coincide. Read through the list, and choose the words to personalize a list for your students. All of the words are taken out of the Narnia books. The next two pages give an overview and example of a completed word analysis.

Show the students where the resources are kept, and make sure they are easily accessible for the necessary research. Below is a list of possible resources along with some Internet links that may prove helpful if all of the suggested resources are not available for your students in print form.

Possible Resource List:

- ✧ *Webster's 1828 Dictionary*
- ✧ Another good dictionary, preferably at high school or college level
- ✧ Thesaurus
- ✧ Bible
- ✧ Bible concordance
- ✧ Dictionary of Etymology (Barnhart is recommended)
- ✧ Any other resource that would help your students with prefixes, suffixes, root words, and definitions

Website Links (accessed August 2011)
- ✧ http://www.litquotes.com/quote_search.php to find a vocabulary word used in classical work of literature
- ✧ http://1828.mshaffer.com/ *Webster's 1828 Dictionary*
- ✧ http://www.etymonline.com/index.php? online etymology dictionary

Do the first word analysis with your students. Model for them how to find the answers. Ensure that your expectations are clear regarding how much of the analysis they are to complete and when the analysis is due. Speed and quantity are not the goals with this type of study. Insist on quality and comprehension.

Analyzing Words

The Magician's Nephew

1	indignant
2	adept
5	principal
5	deplorable
5	minion
8	brandish
8	impertinent
8	vengeance
9	ostentatious
9	abominably
10	merriment
11	desolate
11	violence
14	cunning

word lists by book, and what chapter the word came from

The Lion, the Witch and the Wardrobe

1	inquisitive
2	melancholy
3	accord
4	dominion
5	consideration
6	fraternizing
7	beckoned
8	stratagem
9	ventured
10	solemn
11	repulsive
12	schemes
13	summon
14	triumph

The Horse and His Boy

1	loquacity
3	cultivated
6	avouch
7	diminish
8	skulked
9	luxurious
15	scullion
	victualled

8	placid
	discernment
	maleficence
	irrefutable
	sapient
	vehement
	impetuosity
	imperil
	carbuncles
	wretched
	apophthegms
	decorum
	interminable

Because of the conversation in Chapter 8, there was a vast amount of rich vocabulary. Lewis had fun with this chapter!

Analyzing Words

Use this word analysis to the extent that will best fit your student. Younger students may not be able to research and fill out the entire study without help. This type of in-depth study will teach the student valuable study and research skills and will ensure they internalize and own the knowledge.

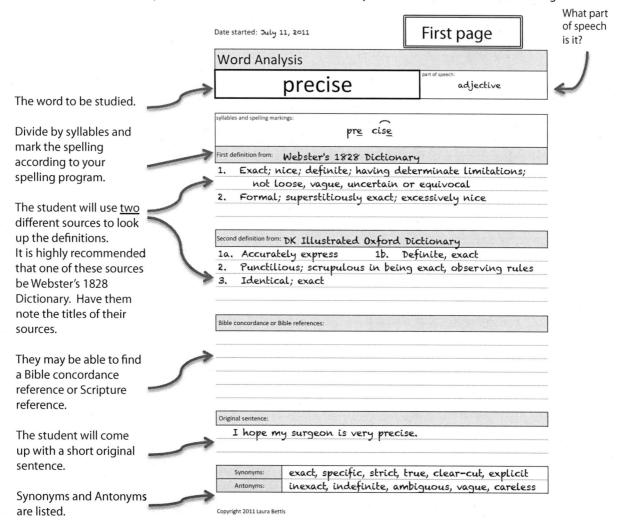

The word to be studied.

Divide by syllables and mark the spelling according to your spelling program.

The student will use two different sources to look up the definitions. It is highly recommended that one of these sources be Webster's 1828 Dictionary. Have them note the titles of their sources.

They may be able to find a Bible concordance reference or Scripture reference.

The student will come up with a short original sentence.

Synonyms and Antonyms are listed.

Date started: July 11, 2011

First page

What part of speech is it?

Word Analysis

precise

part of speech: adjective

syllables and spelling markings:
pre̲ cis̲e

First definition from: Webster's 1828 Dictionary
1. Exact; nice; definite; having determinate limitations; not loose, vague, uncertain or equivocal
2. Formal; superstitiously exact; excessively nice

Second definition from: DK Illustrated Oxford Dictionary
1a. Accurately express   1b. Definite, exact
2. Punctilious; scrupulous in being exact, observing rules
3. Identical; exact

Bible concordance or Bible references:

Original sentence:
I hope my surgeon is very precise.

Synonyms: exact, specific, strict, true, clear-cut, explicit
Antonyms: inexact, indefinite, ambiguous, vague, careless

Copyright 2011 Laura Bettis

They may not be able to fill in everything from each source. That is fine. Filling in the boxes is not the objective. The goal is to get the student to see more deeply into the word. Every portion need not be filled in to accomplish that.

Feel free to copy the blank word analysis sheet and use to assign other words of your choice. As they research and study the word, they may come across another word that they are unfamiliar with, such as: *determinate* or *equivocal* from the definition above. They could begin a word study on that word as well. However, do not give the the student so many words that he is exasperated by this effort. You may wish to make copies of the blank one and have the student keep all of his word studies alphabetized in a notebook.

Give them the vocabulary so they can think the thought!

Analyzing Words

This second page would be for the true word enthusiast. Older students who are capable of digging deeper may find this second page a challenge. Again, the goal is not to have *something* in each box, but to research and think about the meaning in order to fully *own* the knowledge.

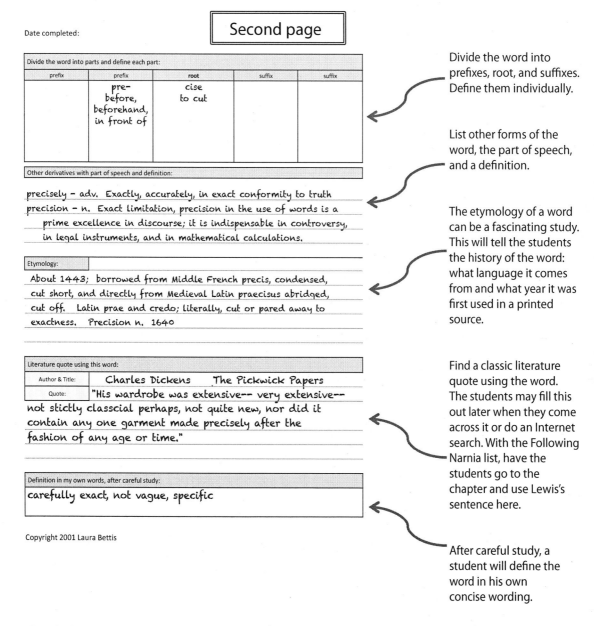

Date completed:

Second page

Divide the word into parts and define each part:

prefix	prefix	root	suffix	suffix
	pre- before, beforehand, in front of	cise to cut		

Other derivatives with part of speech and definition:

precisely – adv. Exactly, accurately, in exact conformity to truth

precision – n. Exact limitation, precision in the use of words is a prime excellence in discourse; it is indispensable in controversy, in legal instruments, and in mathematical calculations.

Etymology:

About 1443; borrowed from Middle French precis, condensed, cut short, and directly from Medieval Latin praecisus abridged, cut off. Latin prae and credo; literally, cut or pared away to exactness. Precision n. 1640

Literature quote using this word:

Author & Title:	Charles Dickens The Pickwick Papers
Quote:	"His wardrobe was extensive-- very extensive--

not stictly classcial perhaps, not quite new, nor did it contain any one garment made precisely after the fashion of any age or time."

Definition in my own words, after careful study:

carefully exact, not vague, specific

Divide the word into prefixes, root, and suffixes. Define them individually.

List other forms of the word, the part of speech, and a definition.

The etymology of a word can be a fascinating study. This will tell the students the history of the word: what language it comes from and what year it was first used in a printed source.

Find a classic literature quote using the word. The students may fill this out later when they come across it or do an Internet search. With the Following Narnia list, have the students go to the chapter and use Lewis's sentence here.

After careful study, a student will define the word in his own concise wording.

A word analysis may take a student one hour to complete both pages. It may take a month. Speed is not of concern, if students are gaining understanding. One word a week or one a month, is fine. They may choose to continue other forms of traditional vocabulary study with the rest of their words and just do a word study for a select few. This is a tool, not a master. However you choose to use this, do the first study or two along with your students, and model for them what you expect.

Give them the vocabulary so they can think the thought!

Date started:

Word Analysis

	part of speech:

syllables and spelling markings:

First definition from:

_____

_____

_____

_____

Second definition from:

_____

_____

_____

_____

Bible concordance or Bible references:

_____

_____

_____

_____

Original sentence:

_____

_____

Synonyms:	
Antonyms:	

Date completed:

Divide the word into parts and define each part:				
prefix	prefix	root	suffix	suffix

Other derivatives with part of speech and definition:

Etymology:

Literature quote using this word:
Author & Title:
Quote:

Concise definition in my own words, after careful study:

Customizable Checklists by IEW Unit

Ultimately, the checklist should be a mental list of structural and stylistic techniques that students can incorporate into each paper they write.

This way they will always have the tools available to polish any paragraph, essay, report, or story they write—now or in the future.

The Student Book contains checklists that are specific to each lesson and include every stylistic technique introduced up to that lesson. In this Teacher's Manual are optional checklists by Unit that are customizable should you prefer to use them. By using these you are able to personalize the checklist to each student. The appropriate Unit checklist should be copied and given to the students before they begin to write from the outline. With the students, review what stylistic techniques you require. Have the students write in the stylistic techniques themselves, as you review it. The checklist should be reviewed beforehand and referenced during writing, not filled in afterwards based on what they ended up using. The requirements should be made clear before they begin.

Stylistic Techniques

EZ+1

Dress-Ups ~ Students should include all the dress-ups that have become easy plus one new one they are practicing.

- Introduction and conclusion paragraphs do not need to include every dress-up. The requirement is lower in these two paragraphs. Let them choose three or so.

Sentence Openers ~ Students should have as much variety in their openers as possible. After they have learned three sentence openers or more, require that they do not have more than two in a row of any kind.

- After they have learned several openers, they should use at least one of each, as possible, in every paragraph. *As possible* means: If a paragraph has five sentences, students must strive to use five different openers unless the inclusion of, for example, a #4 -ing opener strongly interferes with the sensibility of the paragraph.
- If they have an -ly word opener (#3), it does not also count as an -ly word dress-up. Dress-ups are in the middle of a sentence. Openers are at the start of a sentence.

Decorations ~ The requirement for decorations is different from dress-ups and openers. Rather than include all the decorations they know in each paragraph, students should use one or two decorations per paragraph. Any more than that is just cluttering up the paragraph. If they know more than one decoration, rotate your requirements so they get practice with each one, not just their favorite.

Structure

The structure side is filled out with the *basics* of each unit. There are some extra lines if you would like to add in anything else. This side should also be reviewed before the students begin. Remind them of the topic/clincher rule or any other element that is new with the unit.

Marking the Paper

This part is optional, but it does help with accountability.
- Dress-ups are underlined, one of each in each paragraph. Indicate with the abbreviation out in the right-hand margin. If students use four strong verbs, they only need to underline and indicate one.
- Sentence openers are labeled in the left-hand margin with the appropriate number. Students should number all the sentences, to include sentences that start with subject openers. If they only mark the others, they may not see how many subject openers in a row they have.
- Decorations are indicated by dotted underline. Write "DEC." in the margin.
- The words in the topic sentence and clincher sentence that repeat or reflect should be highlighted. If it is an assignment with more than one paragraph, have them use a different color with each paragraph.

Unit 2: _____

Formatting, mechanics, and structural elements are required as listed. Personalize stylistic elements by listing the ones that can be easily incorporated plus one new element.

EZ+1

Structure

Structural Model

❑ Followed structural model

Formatting

❑ I tested my outline aloud
❑ Title centered and underlined
❑ Name
❑ Paragraph indented
❑ Double spaced
❑ _____
❑ _____

Mechanics

❑ Used complete sentences
❑ Punctuation
❑ Capitalization
❑ Spelling
❑ _____
❑ _____

Style

Dress-Ups

No banned words ❑
_____ ❑
_____ ❑
_____ ❑
_____ ❑
_____ ❑
_____ ❑

Sentence Openers

_____ ❑
_____ ❑
_____ ❑
_____ ❑
_____ ❑
_____ ❑

Decorations

_____ ❑
_____ ❑
_____ ❑
_____ ❑
_____ ❑
_____ ❑

Unit 3: _____

Formatting, mechanics, and structural elements are required as listed. Personalize stylistic elements by listing the ones that can be easily incorporated plus one new element.

EZ+1

Structure

Structural Model

- ❑ Followed structural model
- ❑ Title from story clincher

Formatting

- ❑ I tested my outline aloud
- ❑ Title centered and underlined
- ❑ Name
- ❑ Paragraph indented
- ❑ Double spaced
- ❑ _____
- ❑ _____

Mechanics

- ❑ Used complete sentences
- ❑ Punctuation
- ❑ Capitalization
- ❑ Spelling
- ❑ _____
- ❑ _____

Stylistic Elements

	CHARACTERS & SETTING ¶1	PLOT & CONFLICT ¶2	CLIMAX & RESOLUTION ¶3
Dress-Ups			
No banned words	❑	❑	❑
_____	❑	❑	❑
_____	❑	❑	❑
_____	❑	❑	❑
_____	❑	❑	❑
_____	❑	❑	❑
_____	❑	❑	❑
Sentence Openers			
_____	❑	❑	❑
_____	❑	❑	❑
_____	❑	❑	❑
_____	❑	❑	❑
_____	❑	❑	❑
_____	❑	❑	❑
Decorations			
_____	❑	❑	❑
_____	❑	❑	❑
_____	❑	❑	❑
_____	❑	❑	❑
_____	❑	❑	❑
_____	❑	❑	❑

Units 4, 5, and 6: _____

Formatting, mechanics, and structural elements are required as listed. Personalize stylistic elements by listing the ones that can be easily incorporated plus one new element.

Structure

Structural Model

- ❏ Followed structural model
- ❏ Topic and clincher repeat or reflect 2–3 key words
- ❏ Title from final clincher

Formatting

- ❏ I tested my outline aloud
- ❏ Title centered and underlined
- ❏ Name
- ❏ Paragraph indented
- ❏ Double spaced
- ❏ _____
- ❏ _____

Mechanics

- ❏ Used complete sentences
- ❏ Punctuation
- ❏ Capitalization
- ❏ Spelling
- ❏ _____
- ❏ _____

Stylistic Elements

Dress-Ups

- _No banned words_ ❏
- _____ ❏
- _____ ❏
- _____ ❏
- _____ ❏
- _____ ❏
- _____ ❏

Sentence Openers

- _____ ❏
- _____ ❏
- _____ ❏
- _____ ❏
- _____ ❏
- _____ ❏

Decorations

- _____ ❏
- _____ ❏
- _____ ❏
- _____ ❏
- _____ ❏
- _____ ❏

Units 7 and 8: _____

Formatting, mechanics, and structural elements are required as listed. Personalize stylistic elements by listing the ones that can be easily incorporated plus one new element.

Structure

Structural Model

❑ Introduction has a dramatic opening

❑ Body paragraphs each have topic/clincher

❑ Conclusion

❑ Title from final clincher

Formatting

❑ I tested my outline aloud

❑ Title centered and underlined

❑ Name

❑ Paragraph indented

❑ Double spaced

❑ _____

❑ _____

Mechanics

❑ Used complete sentences

❑ Punctuation

❑ Capitalization

❑ Spelling

❑ _____

❑ _____

Stylistic Elements

	INTRODUCTION ¶1	BODY PARAGRAPH ¶2	BODY PARAGRAPH ¶3	BODY PARAGRAPH ¶4	CONCLUSION ¶5
Dress-Ups					
No banned words	❑	❑	❑	❑	❑
_____	❑	❑	❑	❑	❑
_____	❑	❑	❑	❑	❑
_____	❑	❑	❑	❑	❑
_____	❑	❑	❑	❑	❑
_____	❑	❑	❑	❑	❑
_____	❑	❑	❑	❑	❑
Sentence Openers					
_____	❑	❑	❑	❑	❑
_____	❑	❑	❑	❑	❑
_____	❑	❑	❑	❑	❑
_____	❑	❑	❑	❑	❑
_____	❑	❑	❑	❑	❑
_____	❑	❑	❑	❑	❑
Decorations					
_____	❑	❑	❑	❑	❑
_____	❑	❑	❑	❑	❑
_____	❑	❑	❑	❑	❑
_____	❑	❑	❑	❑	❑
_____	❑	❑	❑	❑	❑
_____	❑	❑	❑	❑	❑

It is not necessary for the introduction and conclusion paragraphs to have all the dress-ups. Choose 2–3. However, always vary the sentence openers.

Units 7 and 8: (more than five paragraphs) _____

Formatting, mechanics, and structural elements are required as listed. Personalize stylistic elements by listing the ones that can be easily incorporated plus one new element.

EZ+1

Structure

Structural Model

- ❏ Introduction has a dramatic opening
- ❏ Body paragraphs each have topic/clincher
- ❏ Conclusion
- ❏ Title from final clincher

Formatting

- ❏ I tested my outline aloud
- ❏ Title centered and underlined
- ❏ Name
- ❏ Paragraph indented
- ❏ Double spaced
- ❏ _____
- ❏ _____

Mechanics

- ❏ Used complete sentences
- ❏ Punctuation
- ❏ Capitalization
- ❏ Spelling
- ❏ _____
- ❏ _____

Stylistic Elements

	INTRODUCTION ¶1	BODY PARAGRAPH ¶2	BODY PARAGRAPH ¶3	BODY PARAGRAPH ¶4	BODY PARAGRAPH ¶5	BODY PARAGRAPH ¶6	BODY PARAGRAPH ¶7	CONCLUSION ¶8

Dress-Ups

	INTRODUCTION ¶1	BODY PARAGRAPH ¶2	BODY PARAGRAPH ¶3	BODY PARAGRAPH ¶4	BODY PARAGRAPH ¶5	BODY PARAGRAPH ¶6	BODY PARAGRAPH ¶7	CONCLUSION ¶8
No banned words	❏	❏	❏	❏	❏	❏	❏	❏
_____	❏	❏	❏	❏	❏	❏	❏	❏
_____	❏	❏	❏	❏	❏	❏	❏	❏
_____	❏	❏	❏	❏	❏	❏	❏	❏
_____	❏	❏	❏	❏	❏	❏	❏	❏
_____	❏	❏	❏	❏	❏	❏	❏	❏
_____	❏	❏	❏	❏	❏	❏	❏	❏

Sentence Openers

_____	❏	❏	❏	❏	❏	❏	❏	❏
_____	❏	❏	❏	❏	❏	❏	❏	❏
_____	❏	❏	❏	❏	❏	❏	❏	❏
_____	❏	❏	❏	❏	❏	❏	❏	❏
_____	❏	❏	❏	❏	❏	❏	❏	❏
_____	❏	❏	❏	❏	❏	❏	❏	❏

Decorations

_____	❏	❏	❏	❏	❏	❏	❏	❏
_____	❏	❏	❏	❏	❏	❏	❏	❏
_____	❏	❏	❏	❏	❏	❏	❏	❏
_____	❏	❏	❏	❏	❏	❏	❏	❏
_____	❏	❏	❏	❏	❏	❏	❏	❏
_____	❏	❏	❏	❏	❏	❏	❏	❏

It is not necessary for the introduction and conclusion paragraphs to have all the dress-ups. Choose 2–3. However, always vary the sentence openers.

Unit 9: _____

Formatting, mechanics, and structural elements are required as listed. Personalize stylistic elements by listing the ones that can be easily incorporated plus one new element.

EZ+1

Structure

Structural Model

❑ Introduction has a dramatic opening

❑ Conclusion

❑ Title from final clincher

Formatting

❑ I tested my outline aloud

❑ Title centered and underlined

❑ Name

❑ Paragraph indented

❑ Double spaced

❑ _____

❑ _____

Mechanics

❑ Used complete sentences

❑ Punctuation

❑ Capitalization

❑ Spelling

❑ _____

❑ _____

Stylistic Elements

	INTRODUCTION ¶1	CHARACTERS/ SETTING ¶2	PLOT/CONFLICT ¶3	CLIMAX/ RESOLUTION ¶4	CONCLUSION ¶5

Dress-Ups

	¶1	¶2	¶3	¶4	¶5
No banned words	❑	❑	❑	❑	❑
_____	❑	❑	❑	❑	❑
_____	❑	❑	❑	❑	❑
_____	❑	❑	❑	❑	❑
_____	❑	❑	❑	❑	❑
_____	❑	❑	❑	❑	❑
_____	❑	❑	❑	❑	❑

Sentence Openers

	¶1	¶2	¶3	¶4	¶5
_____	❑	❑	❑	❑	❑
_____	❑	❑	❑	❑	❑
_____	❑	❑	❑	❑	❑
_____	❑	❑	❑	❑	❑
_____	❑	❑	❑	❑	❑
_____	❑	❑	❑	❑	❑

Decorations

	¶1	¶2	¶3	¶4	¶5
_____	❑	❑	❑	❑	❑
_____	❑	❑	❑	❑	❑
_____	❑	❑	❑	❑	❑
_____	❑	❑	❑	❑	❑
_____	❑	❑	❑	❑	❑
_____	❑	❑	❑	❑	❑

It is not necessary for the introduction and conclusion paragraphs to have all the dress-ups. Choose 2–3. However, always vary the sentence openers.

Response to Literature: _____

Formatting, mechanics, and structural elements are required as listed. Personalize stylistic elements by listing the ones that can be easily incorporated plus one new element.

Structure

Structural Model

- ❏ Introduction has a dramatic opening
- ❏ Analysis paragraphs have topic/clincher
- ❏ Conclusion
- ❏ Title from final clincher

Formatting

- ❏ I tested my outline aloud
- ❏ Title centered and underlined
- ❏ Name
- ❏ Paragraph indented
- ❏ Double spaced
- ❏ _____
- ❏ _____

Mechanics

- ❏ Used complete sentences
- ❏ Punctuation
- ❏ Capitalization
- ❏ Spelling
- ❏ _____
- ❏ _____

Stylistic Elements

	INTRODUCTION ¶1	STORY SEQUENCE ¶2	ANALYSIS ¶3	ANALYSIS ¶4	CONCLUSION ¶5
Dress-Ups					
No banned words	❏	❏	❏	❏	❏
_____	❏	❏	❏	❏	❏
_____	❏	❏	❏	❏	❏
_____	❏	❏	❏	❏	❏
_____	❏	❏	❏	❏	❏
_____	❏	❏	❏	❏	❏
_____	❏	❏	❏	❏	❏
Sentence Openers					
_____	❏	❏	❏	❏	❏
_____	❏	❏	❏	❏	❏
_____	❏	❏	❏	❏	❏
_____	❏	❏	❏	❏	❏
_____	❏	❏	❏	❏	❏
_____	❏	❏	❏	❏	❏
Decorations					
_____	❏	❏	❏	❏	❏
_____	❏	❏	❏	❏	❏
_____	❏	❏	❏	❏	❏
_____	❏	❏	❏	❏	❏
_____	❏	❏	❏	❏	❏
_____	❏	❏	❏	❏	❏

It is not necessary for the introduction and conclusion paragraphs to have all the dress-ups. Choose 2–3. However, always vary the sentence openers.

Sample Compositions

Here are some examples of different lessons. These compositions have been written by children of IEW friends and by my own children. They are sorted by lesson number.

Lesson 2

<u>Lost in Its Greed</u>

by Abigail W. (age 10)

Sentence Openers		Dress-Ups & Decorations
		QA
1	The <u>learned</u> Plato once told a Greek myth of a city that had been lost	
1	on account of its greed, the lost city of Atlantis. Poseidon was the wise	
1	god of the sea. He divided one of his greatest islands, Atlantis, into	
1	portions for each of his ten sons. His oldest, King Atlas, received the finest	
1, 1	portion of all. The rest was given to the nine princes. Atlantis was *as round*	*simile*
	as an orange, with <u>jagged</u> mountains, lush, flowery meadows, flowing	QA
	rivers, and <u>treacherous</u> cliffs that <u>plummeted</u> <u>steeply</u> down to the choppy	QA, SV, -ly
4	ocean. Bustling sea-ports, massive stone bridges, people-filled cities, and	
1	elegant castles thrived on the fertile island. The Atlanteans were	
	intelligent, very rich, and were capable of constructing advanced	
3	technology. Unfortunately, these wealthy people <u>greedily</u> longed for	-ly
1	more money and more treasure. Poseidon was furious with the <u>covetous</u>	QA
	island, and as a punishment for their actions, the harsh god stirred up the	
5	sea, and the great city of Atlantis was swallowed overnight! Even though	
1	the Atlanteans had riches beyond compare, they were not satisfied. The	
	superb island city of Atlantis was <u>unquestionably</u> lost in its greed.	-ly

Some of the samples have all of the dress-ups underlined, so students can see the possibilities. When your students mark their own papers, they should underline and indicate just one of each dress-up.

Lesson 3

No One to Rule

by Ben Thomas, age 10, 4th grade

6, 2	Charn was beautiful. Although <u>presently</u> bleak and dreary, at one time its grandeur	-ly
3	and elegance could be <u>compared</u> with no other city. Daily people milled about, content	sv
6, 5	with their lives, except for me. I desired to be queen. As long as my sister, <u>who</u> sat on the	w/w
6, 4	throne, ruled Charn, peace could not exist. I would not allow it. Desiring to remove her	
1	from the throne, I quietly built a <u>militant</u> army. A traitor must have existed amidst my	adj
	ranks, <u>because</u> my sister learned of my plot shortly <u>after</u> I had informed my troops about	b/c, www
	my plan.	

5, 2   When my sister confronted me, I angrily <u>refused</u> to submit to her rule. In my   sv

6   opinion, the only way to peace was my ascension to the throne. I explained this to her.

1, 3, 1   Had she agreed, I would have spared her life. Foolishly, she scoffed at me. We fought

4   <u>until</u> the river of Charn flowed red with the blood of our armies. Breaking her promise,   www

1   my sister, <u>who</u> desperately desired the kingdom, employed <u>powerful</u> magic. How can one   w/w, adj

6, 6, 6   <u>successfully</u> fight magic with men? You cannot. It is impossible. I had no choice. I had   -ly

1   more magic than her <u>because</u> I knew the secret of the Deplorable Word.   b/c

1   The last great battle, <u>which</u> continued for three days, occurred in front of Charn   w/w

2, 1, 6   itself. Not until the end did I use my magic. My men fought to the death. I alone

4   remained. Standing on this terrace, I waited <u>as</u> my sister <u>slowly</u>, yet <u>purposefully</u>   www, dual -ly

5   <u>ascended</u> the <u>spiral</u> staircase before me. When I glimpsed the whites of her eyes, I knew I   sv, adj

3   could not endure under her rule. Suddenly, <u>because</u> I was surrounded, I closed my eyes   b/c

6, 6   tightly and spat the Deplorable Word. Victory finally came. I now ruled Charn. All was

1   perfect, but for one thing: there was no one to rule over.

Lesson 5

Catastrophic Events

by Max Eanes (age 12)

There were many **tragic events** in **London's** history. In 842, perilous Vikings viciously attacked the city. London remained in turmoil until Alfred the Great defeated them in 878. The Vikings returned in 1013 until they fled because Edward the Confessor kicked them out. Sadly, Edward died in 1066, so his nephew, William, took over the throne. Devastating London, the black plague killed one out of three Europeans in 1348. Then World War II occurred. It was horrifying. It seemed interminable. It caused despair. Children were evacuated to the serene countryside, away from powerful, plummeting bombs, to protect them. Even though **London** had many **catastrophic events,** it is now one of the foremost cities in the world.

Lesson 9

The Bad-Tempered Princess

by Gabby Lyon (age 8)

Furiously, the **princess threw** her **scepter** at the **cook**. Her parents gasped in horror as

the scepter struck him right between the eyes. "Oof!" he exclaimed as he spun around and

dropped to the floor. "Humpf!" she sighed. "Elizabeth, I cannot believe my eyes! Why would

you do such a thing?" screamed the king. "He didn't cook my steak correctly," replied the

princess. Sternly, the queen responded, "That may be, but that is no reason for **you** to **throw**

your **scepter** at the **cook**!"

A younger student can write with Unit 5 Writing with Pictures and not use the flashback technique.
That is perfectly fine. Unit 5 is a favorite of all ages. Introduce the flashback when your student is
ready.

Lesson 9

A Golden Transformation

by Jordan Lyon (age 10)

Frustrated with her **horse**, Enchanting, Queen Hera **threw** her **staff**, striking the horse right between its ears. Hera loved this horse and meant it no harm, but now the horse lay hurt and bleeding. Although Hera possessed some power, she did not have the ability to heal the horse. She cast a spell on the horse to turn the ugly black staff into a beautiful golden horn. Her horse was now more wonderful than ever. She now called her **horse** a unicorn, and its beauty reminded her of the day she **threw** her **staff** in anger.

Lesson 9

Key Word Outline:

I. Jadis, iron, bar
    1. Charn, Empress, desolate
    2. P & D, woke, out
    3. iron, bar, London
    4. Digory, Narnia, Aslan
Clincher: Jadis, kill, lion

Paragraph:

The Iron Bar

By Olivia R. (age 10)

Jadis, who had broken an **iron bar** from a lamp-post in London and pitched it at Aslan, had been the wicked Empress of Charn. She had cast a spell that made that world desolate. Polly and Digory had happened upon that world by magic and had accidentally woken her out of an enchanted sleep. She had followed them out of her world and into theirs. Polly and Digory lived in London, and when the Queen arrived, she had yanked an iron bar off of a lamp-post to use as a new weapon. Digory had grabbed her ankle and had dragged her into the new world that was to become Narnia, which Aslan was going to create. Cruelly she had thought that she could kill the lion with the **iron bar.**

Lesson 10

by Joey Bettis (age 9)

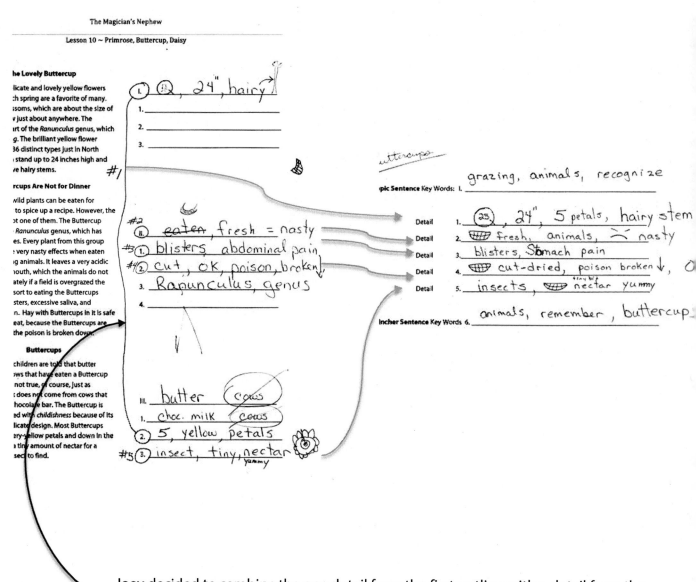

The Magician's Nephew

Lesson 10 ~ Primrose, Buttercup, Daisy

he Lovely Buttercup

licate and lovely yellow flowers
ch spring are a favorite of many.
ssoms, which are about the size of
v just about anywhere. The
rt of the *Ranunculus* genus, which
g. The brilliant yellow flower
36 distinct types just in North
stand up to 24 inches high and
ve hairy stems.

rcups Are Not for Dinner

wild plants can be eaten for
to spice up a recipe. However, the
t one of them. The Buttercup
Ranunculus genus, which has
es. Every plant from this group
very nasty effects when eaten
g animals. It leaves a very acidic
outh, which the animals do not
ately if a field is overgrazed the
sort to eating the Buttercups
sters, excessive saliva, and
n. Hay with Buttercups in it is safe
eat, because the Buttercups are
the poison is broken down.

Buttercups

children are told that butter
ws that have eaten a Buttercup
not true, of course, just as
does not come from cows that
hocolate bar. The Buttercup is
ed with *childishness* because of its
licate design. Most Buttercups
ery-yellow petals and down in the
tiny amount of nectar for a
sect to find.

#1

I. ② , 24", hairy
1. _____
2. _____
3. _____

#2 II. eaten, fresh = nasty
#3 1. blisters abdominal pain
#4 2. cut, OK, poison, broken
3. Ranunculus, genus
4. _____

III. butter (cows)
1. choc. milk (cows)
2. 5, yellow, petals
#5 3. insect, tiny, nectar
yummy

buttercups

pic Sentence Key Words: I. grazing, animals, recognize

Detail 1. ㉕ , 24", 5 petals, hairy stem
Detail 2. fresh, animals, nasty
Detail 3. blisters, Stomach pain
Detail 4. cut-dried, poison broken ↓ , O
Detail 5. insects, nectar yummy
tiny bit

ncher Sentence Key Words 6. animals, remember, buttercup

Joey decided to combine the one detail from the first outline with a detail from the third outline. Then he put the other lines he wanted to keep in order by number. He then transferred the key words to the final fused outline and added a topic and clincher.

He left off a lot of the information that he had taken notes on. Combining some of the remaining details in a logical order gave him a nice arrangement of information for his topic.

Bad Buttercups

by Joey Bettis (age 9)

Because of the buttercup's nasty taste and other effects, animals which have eaten the buttercup flower will recognize it and remember not to eat it. The yellow buttercup has a blossom about the size of a quarter. It grows about 24 inches tall and has hairy stems. When an animal eats a fresh buttercup, it will leave a very nasty taste on an animal's tongue and will give them stinging blisters and terrible stomach pain. But when they are cut and dried, like in a roll of hay, the poison is broken down and is ok to eat. Interestingly, some determined insects will be able to go in the middle and get some yummy nectar without the nasty side effects. After an animal has eaten the buttercup once, it will remember never to make the same mistake again.

The Evacuation

by Seth Stockner (age 12)

September 1939, the evacuation began. Hundreds and thousands of children were sent away from their homes. Teachers sent home a list of things that the children would need. They would need a gas mask, clothing, and a favorite toy to play with. By 1945, 1.5 million children had been evacuated from London. Some of them had starved and had to eat their toothpaste. Some got to see cows for the first time ever. Sadly, some died of sickness, and also some died of starvation. Some children went as far as America and even Canada, and some never got to see their family again. Even though hundreds of children died, the evacuations were successful because they still saved the majority of the children.

Lesson 13

Evacuation Journal Entries
Kyle James Bettis (age 11)
Feb. 2011

September 23, 1939

My name is Johan Shocknoff. My dad gave me this leather bind journal for my 17th birthday. I was so shocked at the fact that all of the children are to be sent away. I started packing my bag with all kinds of supplies to survive this devastating ordeal. The trip took a about a day, and I got some watermelon juice on my face because some kids were throwing fruit around.

September 24, 1939

I finally arrived in the countryside, but on the train ride I met some kid name Peter Pevensie and his three other siblings. It turns out we are going to be neighbors. As the train approached my Great Uncle Howard's massive estate, Michael and I both threw up. After that Uncle Howard met us and showed us around.

April 12, 1941

As I walk downstairs, I see my uncle's massive chandelier and towering plants. Everything in his house is either old or massive or both. After breakfast Michael and I went outside to play and gathered vegetables from the garden. Just then, a whole squadron of planes flew over, and as usual we dove behind some rocks and pretended to shoot them. I think I got one. It makes me wonder how mom and dad are doing back at home in London.

June 12th, 1941

Today at breakfast Uncle Howard told us that he heard that the air-raids had stopped and that we might be going home soon. As soon as I heard, I ran upstairs and started packing! It took me at least a minute to run up all those stairs. As I was packing, I wondered what London would look like after all those bombings. We started loading our luggage onto the train. I hope there aren't any food fights again. The ride took about 6 or 7 hours. I don't really know because the last thing I remember before we arrived was a rotten tomato coming right at me.

Lesson 13
Evacuation Journal Entries
Jordan Moffatt (age 11)
February 2011

September 26, 1939

The red notice I received from my teacher seemed like nothing of any importance, but when I arrived home and saw my mom's face, I knew something was wrong. I had to pack by myself, because all my sisters needed my mom's assistance. When my mom finally told us why we had to pack, there were many tears, but I was glad to have the comfort of my little sisters. Mom made me check the burlap sack several times to make sure I had everything. She also made me pack extra things like a can opener (for the canned food), blankets, and lots of schoolbooks and pencils. Finally that sad day came to an end, but I secretly hoped that the sun would never rise, ever.

September 27, 1939

My wish didn't come true, and the sun rose at its own leisure, and the train arrived to take us away. That morning my mother and I sat together and prayed. When my sisters awoke, they got ready and joined us. I would have to bring the twins Hattie and Jenna, who were 6 months old and the five-year old Alison. Soon after breakfast the train arrived, and we said painful goodbyes to our loving parents and walked onto the train and into a world of troubles and difficulties. On the train was terrifying, as kids were screaming for their parents and would not be comforted. It didn't help that out the back window you could see bombs dropping and London engulfed in flames. When we arrived at the docks, it was no better. Almost half of our food was gone, and we still had to travel to Australia. It was obvious we were starving, but our food was dwindling. I had a lot of comforting to do between the twins and Ali. The twins wouldn't stop bawling the whole time we were on the ship. As the week went on, they got easier to take care of because Ali started to help.

December 8, 1939

Several days before we docked, Hattie started with a fever. We docked in Australia, and a man came up to us and told us he was our new guardian. We followed the man to a large house, where he showed us where we would sleep. The house was finely decorated. It was elegant but still had rooms to play in. Our guardian's name was John Howard. He was charming. His wife, Clarisse, was the sweetest woman I had ever met. She had a smile that made you feel welcomed and safe. Hattie's fever keeps getting worse, and now it's starting to scare me. Mr. John said that we should call a doctor, and we did, but he couldn't help. He said Hattie was doomed.

December 12, 1939

Hattie died last night. Her body was too little to fight off the terrible fever. Even though the day started horribly, the Howards were kind and helped us through the pain, but I ran out of stamps, so now I can't tell Mom. I still can't believe Hattie is gone.

January 2, 1940

I just received a letter from the school's principal in London, saying I cannot ever come home. My parents both perished during a bombing run. I have no idea how to tell Alison. I let Mr. John read the message, and he said that he was very sorry. He told Ali that night at dinner, but he said he had good news too. He said that if we wanted to, we could become Howards and stay with Clarisse and him forever. We had come to love life with the Howards, so we stayed, and Clarisse taught us herself. Even though my old mom died, now I have a happy family.

January 13, 1940

Baby Jenna said her first word today and she called me Sissy. I guess I have time to tell her my real name is Sophie. I think Sissy is good enough for now. Tomorrow is Ali's birthday, and I can't wait to see the look on her face when she sees the ragdoll I made her! Even though I miss my old parents, my new ones are just as splendid and are just as devoted to God as my old ones. So I lost one family but gained a stronger more happy one.

Lesson 13
Evacuation Journal
By Jacqueline Hansen (age 11)
Feb. 2011

September 15ᵗʰ, 1939

    The evacuation began. My teacher sent a note home instructing my mother to pack for the trip to America. At the time, I did not know what was going on. I give the note to my mom and go to my room. Minutes later my mother comes in with a tear-streaked face and sits on my bed. She tells me the situation and then gives me this diary. She tells me that we need to pack for my newborn sister, Claudia and me. She also tells me I am to bring Sherbert, our Golden Retriever, along with me. We pack schoolbooks, including my Bible, blankets, a toy for Claudia, yarn and needles, a gas mask, and a small coin purse with some money. We get canned goods and a can opener, honey, water, smoked meat, corned beef, crackers, bananas, cheese, and bread. I am scared for my family. My mother also gives me letters and stamps to write her. We pray, and I go down to be with my family in the time we have left together. Tomorrow I, Katia Crystal Wilson, will be on the ship, *The Kate*, and will not see my family for a long time.

September 16ᵗʰ, 1939

    My mother woke me early. We had everything downstairs ready to go, but before we left, mother and I had a tea party. It was gorgeous, but it did not last forever. She took Claudia and me down to the train station and kissed us. She put Claudia in her sling and then put it around my shoulders. As we got in the train with our bags, and the train left the station, I saw my mother cry and slowly walk back to our house. Claudia was asleep the whole train ride, but when we got off to get on the boat, she finally awoke. I gave her some milk and banana and she calmed down. As I look up at the ship, *The Kate*, I am in shock. It is a nasty boat. Someone leads me to a room, and I am stunned but still thank him, set down my bags, and give him a tip. He seems to appreciate it very much. I put Claudia on our bed and sit down. I pull out my knitting and start to work on a blanket. While I knit, I think about what this beastly voyage will be like. I say a quick prayer, write a letter home, and go to sleep. It has been a long day. Good night.

November 7th, 1939

We got off the boat and felt relieved that the ground was not moving anymore. We are to stay with our great grandfather, Phillip Reynolds, until it is safe in England again. Our grandfather is too old and sick to pick us up, so we must find our way home. I walk into a shop and ask the owner if he knows where Mr. Phillip Reynolds lives. He said he does and points me in the right direction. When I get there, I knock—but no answer. So I open the door and see a man reading the newspaper near the blistering fire. I put my bags down, and I, with Claudia in my arms, go over near him, and I say, "Sir, we are your great grandchildren, and we are to stay with you." He replies in a cranky, crinkly voice, "You will sleep upstairs." Then with a glare in our direction, he tells me to "go now." I obey and take my bags upstairs. There are three rooms. I choose the biggest out of the rooms that are unoccupied. I set down my bags and Claudia, start to unpack, and eat what we have left, of course saving some for Claudia. The room is as dingy and dusty as the whole house. I'm scared for myself as well as for Claudia, but for now it is dark and I must sleep, for my birthday is in two days, and we will buy some cake. Good night.

May 17th, 1945

After eating cold porridge with Claudia, I went to get mail when I saw a letter written by my mother. I dropped everything else, scurried inside, and got Claudia. I raced to our room and read the letter. Out of the six years we have been here, we have only gotten two letters from our mother. This is the third. What was in it was the best news ever. The war was over! We could come home. I was overjoyed and started packing our belongings. Since grandfather died six months ago, I had been selling eggs to make a living, and we had a garden for food, so this news was even better. In the letter it said she bought us two plane tickets, so we could come home the next week. She also said that she was to have another baby. It was so exciting, and today being Claudia's birthday, she thought it the best birthday present in the world. We had a day of thanking the Lord, praying, and reading the Bible. It was finally the day. The day we go home!

Lesson 14
Character Analysis: The White Witch
Paragraph from Chapters 2–4
by Kyle Bettis (age 12)
January 2012

The **White Witch**, a self-centered and **cunning** woman, had declared herself **Ruler of Narnia**. With her magic she made Narnia always winter, but never Christmas. She commanded that anyone who saw humans was to kidnap them and turn them over to her. As a result of disobedience to this command, anyone who didn't obey would face severe or even deadly consequences. She even looked evil with her face as white as paper or even snow, and her lips blood red. She was proud, cold, and most of all, cruel. Supposedly, she was "Queen of Narnia." When she first approached Edmund, she thought he was an idiotic dwarf. She was very rude, although when she realized he was a human, she was suddenly very sweet and polite. She was being very deceitful, so she could trick him into giving up his sisters and brother. By ensnaring Edmund and his siblings, the cruel, **cunning Queen** hoped to ensure her **grasp on Narnia.**

Lesson 15
Character Analysis: The White Witch
Paragraph from Chapters 6–8
by Kyle Bettis (age 12)
January 2012

The **evil White Witch** was **cruel** and creepy and was crippling Narnia. By her command, the secret police destroyed Mr. Tumnus' house. Unfortunately he had been charged with treason against the White Witch. By doing this, she was warning the other animals in Narnia. Many were on her side. Even some trees were evil. After hearing about Mr. Tumnus, they knew they had to escape. As Mr. Beaver observed the snowfall he explained, "This snow will cover our tracks." He was glad their tracks would be covered so that her spies would not be able to tell which direction they had gone. Mr. When Beaver had looked into Edmund's eyes, he knew that Edmund had been in Narnia before and fallen under her spell. He said that anyone who lives in Narnia could see that. All of these despicable deeds show how **evil** and **cruel** the **White Witch** was.

Lesson 16
Character Analysis: The White Witch
Paragraph from Chapters 9–11
by Kyle Bettis (age 12)
January 2012

Another dastardly **character trait** of the **White Witch** was that she was **ruthless**. According to her actions and directives, it was even clear to Edmund now that she was a ruthless tyrant. The wolves had been instructed by her to kill anyone they saw, and they rushed to the Beavers' house to find their next victims. The White Witch came upon the animals feasting in the woods, and without hesitation she turned them all to stone because they were celebrating. When Edmund sheepishly asked for something to eat, she commanded the dwarf to give Edmund stale bread and water. He refused both. She was furious. He ate. Since it seemed Edmund was taking the side of the animals, he was whacked upon the head by the **ruthless** witch. This concludes the **characteristics** of the **White Witch**.

Lesson 21
Comparison and Contrast of the White Witch and Hitler
First Body Paragraph - Comparing
by Kyle Bettis (age 12)
February 2012

As you are about to see, the White Witch and Hitler are similar in many ways. The evil ruler, the White Witch, is in control of her country, which is parallel to Hitler leading Germany. Cruelly she used fear as a motivational tool to control Narnia. Similarly Hitler used a weak government to his advantage by using fear and persuading the president to make him the chancellor. In the end, they both were defeated. The White Witch was defeated in battle, and Hitler fell in Berlin. As you can plainly see, the White Witch and Hitler have many resemblances.

Lesson 21
Comparison and Contrast of the White Witch and Hitler
Second Body Paragraph: Contrasting
by Kyle Bettis (age 12)
February 2012

The White Witch and Hitler may be similar in many ways, but everyone's different. While they both used fear to gain control, the White Witch took power of Narnia mainly by force, whereas Hitler persuaded Germany's weak president to give him the position of chancellor of Germany. Ironically all the people of Narnia hate her, whereas Hitler's people eventually supported him and even cheered for him. In the end the White Witch was killed by Aslan during battle, which is quite the opposite of Hitler's demise. Hitler saw the end coming and took his own life. As you can see, the White Witch and Hitler have many contrasting qualities.

Cruel Intentions

by Jacqueline Hansen (age 12)

They are rulers of their countries, but they are detested and feared. These two cruel creatures are Adolf Hitler and the White Witch. They both deceived their way to leadership, are convincing, influential, and deceitful speakers, and are greedy, self-centered, and dominating rulers. They also have many differences. The White Witch started conquering immediately, enslaving everyone, while using her magic. Hitler focused on indoctrinating the children and threatening and deceiving the adults, until he slowly became the leader. Both the White Witch's and Hitler's rules ended in catastrophe because they began with wicked intentions.

The malicious White Witch and the cruel Adolf Hitler conquer and rule in similar ruthless, vicious, and self-absorbed ways. The White Witch is a convincing speaker when she persuades Edmund that he deserves more power and offers it to him. Hitler convinces the German people that they deserve better treatment after WWI and gives them hope. The White Witch acts greedily when she enslaves everyone and takes over Narnia. Hitler behaves selfishly when he threatens the president and finally dominates Germany. The majority would not have chosen either the White Witch or Hitler to be their leader. The Narnians disapproved of, hated, and feared the White Witch. Hitler did not earn enough votes to be elected. Hitler and the White Witch exhibit the same evil through manipulation, enslavement, and self-centeredness.

The White Witch and Hitler have many differences in the ways they took power and rule their countries. The White Witch started conquering immediately, while Hitler tried multiple times before he gained power, even going to jail in between attempts. Hitler raised the children to be a loyal generation of followers through public school while the White Witch went after everyone and brutally forced them to serve her. The White Witch used magic to coerce the people to submission while Hitler used deceit, cruel manipulation, and eventually force. The White Witch and Hitler used different ways to overtake their countries and subjugate their people.

The iniquitous White Witch and the pernicious Adolf Hitler have many similarities but are still different. They are both self-centered, deceitful, and influential speakers whose lives were driven by greed. The White Witch immediately conquered, deceived, and enslaved the Narnians. Hitler manipulated through threats and deception and then conquered and subjugated the Germans. When greed runs your life you will not succeed. Both autonomous, evil leaders were defeated; the White Witch by Aslan, the kings and the Narnians and Hitler by the Allies of WWII. Proverbs 15:27 tells us, "Whoever is greedy for unjust gain troubles his own household, but he who hates bribes will live." If you proceed with ruthless and cruel intentions, you will fail.

Jacqui's KWO

I. WW & H rulers, malicious, nefarious, hateful, selfish

    1. Similarities: convincing, influential, greedy, self-centered, ~~chosen~~

    2. Differences: conquering: WW-immediate, H-slowly, target to deceive: WW-everyone, H-children, power: WW-magic, H-manipulation

    3. Evil intent, deceit, domination = loses

II. Topic sentence: WW & H, vicious, ruthless similar

    1. Idea 1 WW: convincing speaker, deserved better, Edmund, offer hope

    2. Idea 1 H: convincing speaker, deserved better German people, offer hope

    3. Idea 2 WW: greedy, enslaving, took over

    4. Idea 2 H: greedy, threatening, enslaving

    5. Idea 3 WW: majority ~~chosen~~, hated, feared

    6. Idea 3 H: majority ~~votes~~

Clincher: H & WW evil - ruthless, similar manip., slaving, selfish

III. Topic sentence: WW & H, differences rule & take power

    1. Idea 1 WW: started conquering immediately

    2. Idea 1 H: tried multiple Xs, 4 power, jail

    3. Idea 2 WW: wanted, everyone 2 B follower

    4. Idea 2 H: raised children 2 B followers

    5. Idea 3 WW: forced leadership magic

    6. Idea 3 H: forced leadership. manipulation, deceit

Clincher: H & WW diff. techniques 2 overtake, subjugate

IV. WW & H have similarities but differences

    1. Both gifted speakers, self-centered, deceitful, greed-most

    2. WW- conquered, deceived, & enslaved; H-threatened, manip, deceived, & subjugated, conquered

    3. Evil never wins, both overthrown; H-WWII defeated, WW-defeated by Aslan, Kings & Narnians

    4. Prov. 15:27 "Whoever is greedy for unjust gain troubles his own household, but he who hates bribery will live."

    5. Evil intent, deceit, domination = loses

Lesson 26

Character Analysis of Shasta – KWO

by Julia Hansen (age 13)   (Julia put her outline on her own paper, so she would have more room for all her ideas, until she knew what she wanted to choose to go in her paragraph.)

Topic sentence: Who is the character?

    Shasta, longing, fearful, accommodating, eagerness

Qualities of Shasta: Reliable ~ packed immediately

        Diligent ~ carried out decision to leave, got up from falls

        Fearful ~ when Tarken wanted to buy him, father

        Arrogant, rude ~ judging the girl, laughs at horse for lying down

        Childish ~ daydreaming, wasting time, fussed about breakfast

        Cooperative ~ worked daily, followed Bree's directions for everything

        Loyal ~ to horse, did not tell of plan to leave

        Trustworthy ~ to horse, did not tell master of talking horse

        Curious ~ daydreaming about other lands, willing to leave immediately

Give examples from book that illustrate chosen quality:

        Loyal ~ to horse by not telling of plans to leave or that he could talk

        Cooperative ~ followed all of horse's guidance, got back on the horse even when tired

How does he feel inside?

    Lonely – alone, father is neglectful, unpredictable (sometimes beating, sometimes non-expressive)

    Longing inside – asks questions about lands, daydreaming

    Agreeable, accommodating – he attempts to do daily work, taught to be submissive – father boxes ears, agrees to run away right now, learns to ride the horse because he's told to, he gets breakfast because the horse suggests it, gets back on the horse because he's told to give up when the Lion is chasing him

    Anxious - stutters when he says he can fall if necessary, during the chase

    Excited- leaves right away, hardly concerned with leaving home, except for Donkey

What was the effect on others or the situation?

    Bree – considers him a friend and believes he's honest, acts as the boy's charge meaning he cares for him and watches over him

(p. 31) "I'll vouch for the boy, Tarkheena. He's been true to me, and a good friend. And he's certainly either a Narnian or an Archenlander."

A Bible verse or favorite quote may go next to illustrate:

    A kind man benefits himself, but a cruel man brings trouble on himself. (Proverbs 11:17)

But the meek will inherit the land and enjoy **peace** and prosperity. (Psalm 37:10-12) (in context)

Clincher Sentence:

    Shasta, curious, obligatory, anxious, longing

Hope for the Humble

by Julia Hansen (age 13)

Shasta is a curious, accommodating, and anxious little boy who drudges through his daily workload dreaming of distant lands when a chance to escape shows itself through a talking horse. Shasta has spent his life constantly asking his neglectful father about what lies in the North. He is curious about a different life away from fishnets, cooking, and cleaning. Shasta has always been agreeable, although somewhat apprehensive and shows this with the horse, Bree. The ideas and requests Bree makes are painlessly accommodated by Shasta. He willingly agrees to leave his home even though he will never see this life again. He helpfully follows Bree's careful instructions about putting on the saddle and training to ride even without holding on. And he cooperates with Bree's decision to travel with company although he doesn't trust the others. Bree responds to Shasta's actions by saying that he will "vouch for the boy … He's been true to me and a good friend" (Chapter 2, p. 31). The Lord says that "the meek will inherit the land and enjoy peace and prosperity" (Psalm 37:10-12). Hope is on the horizon for this humble, obligatory little boy who has always had a longing for adventure.

Selected Bibliography

Benge, Janet & Geoff. *C. S. Lewis Master Storyteller*. Seattle, Washington: YWAM Publishing, 2007.

Daynes, Katie. *Usborne Famous Lives Adolf Hitler*. London, England: Usborne, 2006.

Dowswell, Paul. *The Usborne Introduction to the Second World War*. Tulsa, Oklahoma: EDC Publishing, 2004.

Faber, Harold & Doris. *American Heroes of the 20th Century*. New York: Random House, 1967.

Grambs, David. *The Describer's Dictionary*. New York: W.W. Norton & Company, Inc., 1993.

Grant, R. G. *World War II*. New York: DK, 2008.

Pellegrino, Victor C. *A Writer's Guide*. Hawaii: Maui arThoughts Company, 2004.

Pudewa, Andrew. *Teaching Writing: Structure and Style Syllabus & Seminar Workbook*. Locust Grove, Oklahoma: Institute for Excellence in Writing, L.L.C., 2010.